THE SONG OF
LEONARD
COHEN

THE SONG OF

LEONARD
COHEN

PORTRAIT OF A POET,
A FRIENDSHIP AND A FILM

HARRY RASKY

mosaic press

National Library of Canada Cataloguing in Publication Data

Rasky, Harry, 1928-
    The song of Leonard Cohen

ISBN 0-88962-742-8

I. Cohen, Leonard, 1934 - . 2. Composers - Canada - Biography
3. Singers - Canada - Biography. I. Title

ML410.C69R22 2001   782.42164'092   C00-933135-2

Published by Mosaic Press, offices and warehouse at 1252 Speers Road, Units 1 and 2, Oakville, Ontario, L6L 5N9, Canada and Mosaic Press, PMB 145, 4500 Witmer Industrial Estates, Niagara Falls, NY, 14305-1386, U.S.A.

Mosaic Press acknowledges the assistance of the Canada Council and the Department of Canadian Heritage, Government of Canada for their support of our publishing programme.

Printed and Bound in Canada.
ISBN 0-88962-742-4

MOSAIC PRESS in Canada:
1252 Speers Road, Units 1 & 2,
Oakville, Ontario
L6L 5N9
Phone/Fax: 905-825-2130
mosaicpress@on.aibn.com

MOSAIC PRESS in U.S.A.:
4500 Witmer Industrial Estates
PMB 145, Niagara Falls, NY
14305-1386
Phone/Fax: 1-800-387-8992
mosaicpress@on.aibn.com

Le Conseil des Arts | The Canada Council
du Canada | for the Arts

for Arlene
whose great love is like a song

Films by Harry Rasky

William Hutt: A Most Fortunate Man, 1997
Christopher Plummer: King of Players, 1995
The War Against the Indians, 1992
The Magic Season of Robertson Davies, 1990
The Great Teacher: Northrop Frye, 1989
Degas, 1987-88
To Mend the World, 1986
Karsh: The Searching Eye, 1985-86
The Mystery of Henry Moore, 1985
Raymond Massey: Actor of the Century, 1984
Stratasphere, 1983
The Spies Who Never Were, 1981
Being Different, 1981
The Man Who Hid Anne Frank, 1981
The Song of Leonard Cohen, 1981
Arthur Miller on Home Ground, 1979
The Lessons of History, Will and Ariel Durant, 1978
The Peking Man Mystery, 1977
Homage to Chagall, 1976-77
Travels Through Life with Leacock, 1975
Next Year In Jerusalem, 1974
Baryshnikov, 1974
Tennessee Williams' South, 1973
The Wit and World of G. Bernard Shaw, 1972
Upon This Rock, 1972
Hall of Kings, 1967
Operation Sea War – Vietnam
A Tour of Washington with Mrs. Lyndon Johnson
The Nobel Prize Awards
The Twentieth Century
NBC White Paper – Panama, Danger Zone
Cuba and Castro Today

Books by Harry Rasky

Tennessee Williams: A Portrait in Laughter and Lamentation
The Three Harrys: A Memoir
Stratas: An Affectionate Tribute to Teresa Stratas
Nobody Swings on Sunday: The Many Lives and Films of Harry Rasky

Videocassettes of Harry Rasky's films, *The Song of Leonard Cohen*
and *Tennessee Williams' South* are available from Mosaic Press

ACKNOWLEDGMENTS

In the years since I created the film *The Song of Leonard Cohen*, I would occasionally dust it off in periods of manic melancholy. I always adored the symphonic poem that was the 1979 tour of Leonard Cohen which I was fortunate enough to document in my own style.

The sound of it, the colour of it would last in my memory for weeks. It haunted me. So Leonard never left me.

Through my own musical daughter Holly and son Adam and students of my class at the University of Toronto, I realized that Leonard crossed all time zones. He was a singer for us all.

Along came Howard Aster of Mosaic Press who suggested that somehow it was time to publish all of that — the story, the poems, the lyrics, which composed the film. Amy Land at Mosaic devoted her significant editorial and design to complete this book. In an astonishing remembrance of things past and present, Sony has just now wisely issued a newly minted CD. The film does not lose any of its original tone and texture. So now in 2001 we can again appreciate him.

I thank you Leonard for your sound and your substance and a friendship I treasure.

L'Chaim!

Harry Rasky

The mood seems right. The rhythm
takes hold of me and the music begins.
Now let us share the life that is the
Song of Leonard Cohen

April 16, 2000

I suppose I will never forget the phone call which came so recently from Leonard.

It had truly been the winter of my discontent. Although I had escaped, I thought, to Florida to repair my damaged body, I had not been able to hide from myself. And each day my sense of mortality made me gasp — a mental agony that choked me in the brightness of colors and the monotony of sea sounds. I fled with my always-supportive wife to the safety of Air Canada and the cocoon comfort of home.

But here in Toronto, with its self-righteous smugness, I faced the always-punishing Canadian winter. The wicked winter let go one final blast of frost and snow. If April is truly the cruelest month, I felt its lingering bite.

On such a day, the phone call came — the warmth of Leonard's voice recorded on my answering machine at my Canadian Broadcasting Corporate office, a place cluttered with memory of other poets such as Tennessee Williams and singers of soul like Teresa Stratas. I am a collector of great creative beauty and my office is stacked with their accomplishments. I am humbled by their offerings to us all. They tumble through my mind like the brightly colored figures in a Marc Chagall painting; fantasy and reality and beyond. Beyond the beyond. I praise them now as I did in my films, meditations on God. If God is the great creator, these men and women have tried through paint and passion, words and music to give us this day and every day, personal fragments of their creation. I honor them.

Leonard, the poet, offered simple words in his phone message that April day in the unlikely year 2000.

"Harry this is Leonard. I just wanted you to know I watched your film on me and it struck me I never thanked you enough at the time for the magnificent gift you gave with that film. Call me." Then he left his personal number.

His thanks were not required. The film *The Song of Leonard Cohen* had been one of the creative pleasures of my life, an attempt to blend his poetry and his passion with my own. I do not watch it often because his sound haunts me and it takes days, if not weeks, before I am free of it, if ever.

If there was anything surprising about the call — and I am seldom surprised — is that the film has been finished twenty years earlier and he and I had viewed it together in a Toronto studio one late August afternoon. Twenty years and counting.

I tried to reach him and left my home number. Another call came. This time he said, "Harry I missed a couple digits of your number. Call again. My hearing isn't what it was."

I started to become somewhat neurotic, I think, about the CBC. The once almost great network, which had been home to my satisfying work and the work of others, had become kidnapped by middle managers who showed little possibility for taste. What is worse, films such as the one I made with Leonard had become entombed by bureaucratic thinking, making it virtually impossible to share them with a public craving quality. Wintry thinking was strangling them. So the call became even more important somehow. I responded speaking slowly and loudly, but lovingly.

He called again and spoke to my wife Arlene who has always been shy in his presence. Finally after a week we connected. You see, what I feel about Leonard is that he has become as much myth as man. He is the best poet, or seems to be, the poet we wish we all had the courage to become. We have tracked him as we would Keats or Shelley, enjoying the reported sightings. "Leonard in Tennessee. Leonard up the mountain, Mount Baldy in California. Lately, Leonard in India. Leonard universal sex symbol. Leonard monk and spiritual source."

I sometimes think that Leonard is like Cary Grant who, in his prime said, " Yes, we would all like to be Cary Grant — I wish I were." Over the years I have often thought of him, called him when in Montreal, spoken with him when that was possible, but I have never felt it was necessary to have constant contacts. It's something like the sparrows which live in the caves near my chimney. I rejoice when I hear them in the morning and I delight in them when they show themselves. But I know I could never catch one or want to. But they are "my sparrows." And I am their friend, I am Leonard's friend, I think. But to be, he needs to be free, of course. He has written about it often and sung its praise.

Like a bird on the wire
Like a drunk in a midnight choir
I have tried in my way to be free

And that is how I first found him, all those years ago. It was, as I recall, in 1962. Imagine, almost forty years ago! Let's start then on the sun-parched island of Hydra in Greece.

I can never forget it.

Hydra and the Island of the Mind

> *Anything that moves is white,*
> *a gull, a wave, a sail,*
> *and moves too purely to be aped.*
> *Smash the pain.*

It was that time of our lives. We were, what is called in Yiddish *buchers*, young bucks, first apart and briefly together. For me it was a time of total adventure. For Leonard, a sampling of the delights that life could offer, usually centered around a starkly beautiful sad-smiling young woman. He was a poet in development. All was passion and pain, limited by the words to express the ecstasy and the agony. No music yet, to suffer along with the suffering.

I was returning from a remarkable adventure in Africa, my second time round. My first tour included all of Africa south of the Sahara. Now, I had returned to the magic mountain Kingdom of Ethiopia. I still have the telephone book that covered the entire sheltered feudal nation.

These are some of its listings:

H.I.M. the Empress

> Imperial Palace
> Rubresen Tative
> Steward
> Cashier

H.I.H. the Crown Prince
> Palace
>
> Palace, direct line

H.I.H. the Duke of Harrar

Do not try to call now. They are all either assassinated or in hiding.

Ethiopia at that time looked so much like the land the world forgot. Tucked away on a high plateau, it was the country the explorers chose to ignore, too difficult to conquer in the conquistador days of colonialism.

If the Bible was being relived, that is where it would be happening. So it seemed then, almost forty years ago, when the Emperor was treated like God! Even when he bathed at night alone in his bathtub, if not a divinity, then at least on first name terms with him.

I had filmed for a two part series called The Twentieth Century at CBS, what became, *The Lion and the Cross*. Addis Ababa was delicious. Each street was a scene from Cecil B. DeMille's *Dust and Delight*.

I decided to take the long way home. I felt the need to find Western Civilization all over again. While I had been removed from our great culture President Kennedy had challenged the Soviet Union with the so-called 'missile crisis' and we had been a breath away from obliteration. I had been in one of the few landscapes that never knew. Turn, turn, turn, back to the beginning or close to it. I had no appetite for Africa. I removed myself from the Air Ethiopia plane in Athens, Greece and booked myself on a one-day excursion to the Greek Islands, but found myself abandoning the ferryboat in Hydra, the first stop.

I had always been a lousy tourist. I loved to taste the fabric and reality of the place. Hydra was a solid cliff of houses rising from the sea, white on white with black-draped women, hiding from the sun and glaring eyes of sea-parched hungry men.

This is where I found Leonard. The expatriates from Europe and North America gathered daily at a café on the waterfront to enjoy retsina and shish kebabs and conversation. I was immediately welcomed. Leonard was a starkly beautiful young man sitting perched really with a half smile, chain-smoking cigarettes, and somehow both nervous and relaxed if that is possible.

Speaking quietly, warmly, but not revealing too much. A poem of the time:

> *I dress in black*
> *I have green eyes*
> *In certain light*
>
> *If others try to write this*
> *death to them*
> *death to anyone*
> *if he or she unseal this poem*
> *in which I dress in black*
>
> *and bless your eyes*
> *who hurry from this page*
> *Put a green-eyed man*
> *out of his misery and rage*

Some things can be revealed by the poetry of the time. But mostly it was the struggle to find who he was, who he is.

> *I'd like to read*
> *one of the poems*
> *that drove me into poetry*
> *I can't remember one line*
> *Or where to look*

It is a game he used to play "Don't look for me. I am not there."
He was always there. Born a poet. There was no other way. He was
also, I think, what his name suggests —a *Cohen*— a member of the
select group, the high priests of Israel. He knew it then and now,
even if it came wrapped in its own *talus* of self-doubt.

> *I am a priest of God*
> *I walk down the road*
> *with my pocket in my hand*
> *Sometimes I'm bad*
> *then sometimes I'm very good*
> *I believe that I believe*
> *everything I should*
> *I like to hear you say*
> *when you dance with head rolling*
> *upon a silver tray*
> *that I am a priest of God*

Did I know that then? No. I knew very little about him, truly.
He had come from the literary tradition of Montreal. And the two
solitudes embraced more than the separate languages. Toronto,
my birthplace, and Montreal were miles apart. I knew only he was
considered a visiting star. But a poet what was that, and what did
it have to do with me, a curious wanderer to wars and love? If I
learned anything and I am still uncertain, we were not so far apart—
Leonard, son of priests and grandson of priests and I, son of a cantor
who sang so joyously and with melancholy of the loneliness of God.
Elohim. Shma Yisroel, Adonai Elohaynu, Adonai Echod.

But even then I felt an instant rapport. It is difficult to make
same-sex lasting friendships and I knew immediately that we
would find a place for each other in our passage through life. There
was then and now an instant feeling of gentlemanly caring about
Cohen — not physical but in the matter of the soul. You could

not be casual. The poet's heart would not allow it. The echo of God commanded something deeper. I was welcomed. A poem not yet written. A song not yet sung.

> *One by one the guests arrive*
> *The guests are coming through*
> *The open-hearted many*
> *The broken-hearted few*
>
> *And no one knows where the night is going*
> *And no one knows why the wine is flowing*
> *O love, I need you, I need you, I need you*
> *I need you now*
>
> *And those who dance begin to dance*
> *And those who weep begin*
> *Welcome, welcome cries a voice*
> *Let all my guests come in*
>
> *And no one knows where the night is going*
> *And no one knows why the wine is flowing*
> *Love, I need you, I need you. I need you*
> *I need you now*

There was much wine and much dancing in those autumn nights on Hydra. I discovered the Zorba-the-Greek, sound of bouzoki music. It must have touched the Russian in my soul. Leonard was an involved spectator. The rhythms oozed out of my being at the small café where the emotionally scarred writers and artists gathered. The retsina was flowing. And how I danced!

Around that time his mythical dream-girl, his Swedish companion with whom he had lived the idyllic poet's life in his Hydra house, had left him. She, her spirit really, became enshrined in one of his classic songs of mourning. Leonard was in many ways like a great, eloquent, mourning dove.

Come over to the window, my little darling
I'd like to try to read your palm
I used to think I was some kind of gypsy boy
before I let you take me home

So long, Marianne
it's time that we began
to laugh and cry and laugh
about it all again

You know I love to live with you
but you make me forget so very much
I forget to pray for the angels
and then the angels forget to pray for us

We met when we were almost young
down by the green lilac park
You held on to me like I was a crucifix
as we went kneeling though the dark

Your letters they all say you're beside me now
Then why do I feel so alone
I'm standing on this ledge and your fine spider web
is fastening my ankle to a stone

Now I need your hidden love
I'm cold as a new razor blade
You left when I told you I was curious
I never said that I was brave

O you are really such a pretty one
I see you've gone and changed your name again
And just when I climbed this whole mountainside
to wash my eyelids in the rain

So long Marianne
It's time that we began
To laugh and cry and cry and laugh
About it all again

At the time Leonard was strictly a poet, a haunted, handsome poet. The song was yet to come, at least publicly. The music still in his head, waiting for release. Music to marry his lyrics.

These were Hydra afternoons of pure hashish and the kind of intense conversation that only the impractical unlived can indulge in and consider vital. And perhaps they were. Like forsythia, in their impossible yellows, before the seasons have washed away their innocence and they become matter-of-fact bland green. Who can know for sure?

And the wine was flowing

Each day the tour guide would come by and ask if I was ready to leave this rock of sensuality and pleasure. Each day I would respond — not yet, not quite yet.

Leonard's home, which he had purchased, was halfway up the cliff. It was profoundly white, furnished with the naked essentials, which I have since come to associate with his desire to never show any love of what the rest of the world might call comfort. It was monk-like, on an island that was dominated at its top by a nunnery where the nuns could only be reached by a winding donkey path. They knitted gay, elaborate wool sweaters as the world below unfolded. There was an austere, remote romance about the whole place, parched white on the outside but a heavy breathing of many emotional colors not far below the surface. The Mediterranean was still deliciously unpolluted in those days. And we would set the swimming hour as it suited the time between wine and conversation. Leonard and I have always had a passion for swimming.

In the late, afternoon, before the siesta, the intellectual moveable feast would catch the late sun.

And the wine was flowing

We would play this game. I, as a filmmaker, had always had this large ego sense that the world was revolving around me. So then, when I left, somehow all the world left behind vanished. All places were a kind of Brigadoon. So the game was that when the ferryboat turned the bend, if I were aboard, the island and its residents, our crowd, would cease to exist.

One day, the day came. I would return to New York and begin editing of what became *The Lion and the Cross*. Time to make my way back to Manhattan despite the warning that had been offered by the Cuban Missile Crisis just a few weeks before that the world was, indeed, becoming a much more dangerous place. As the ferry turned the bend I could see the group, clinging to each other and holding onto the furniture, led by Leonard. But, of course, I was mistaken and he remained a gentleman to the end.

We had made plans for a return around the spring. But it would never be the same for me as that autumn when it seemed the world might suddenly be coming to an end, the world of white.

Anything that moves is white,
a gull, a wave, a sail,
and moves too purely to be aped.
Smash the pain.

Never pretend peace.
The consolumentum has not,
never will be kissed. Pain
cannot compromise this light.

Do violence to the pain,
ruin the easy vision,
the easy warning, water
for those who need to burn.

These are ruthless: rooster shriek,
bleached goat skull.
Scalpels grow with poppies
if you see them truly red.

And the forsythia blossoms, torches of yellow youth, were blowing in the wind of the sixties. The striving, driving was everything. Become a hero! Find fame and certainly fortune would follow! And contentment — yes, that illusive thing called happiness! Paradise? It was hard to see the paradise of the here and now, the paradise we hold in our hands, searching for something we thought we held in our hearts. And so it became paradise lost.

There were many markers in Leonard's life, but what did they tell us?

He had been born into a semi-rich family, as many Montreal Jewish families were, seeking stability in the then thriving clothing business.

His great-grandfather, it's been said, was the first Zionist in Canada, with one uncle an OBE and a great-uncle Chief Rabbi.

It was a time when the family had both a governess and chauffeur. It's said that he was the fat little kid no one liked. His father died when he was nine and he became attached more closely to his mother and sister. He felt like a 'beautiful loser.' Irving Layton, the rough and tumble poet rogue, became a substitute father in many ways, a guiding rebel. Was it possible that you could be a Jew and poet and somehow survive in the wilds of Canada?

He would try, succeed in a way, and fail in another way, like a caged bird, always trying to be free, not sure where freedom lay. Certainly his attempt to move into the family business after McGill University was not the way. Trapped by material stuffiness, a month in law school left him hungry for breath. Graduate school at Columbia University where he was advised by a wise professor — this is no way to become a poet. How about the simple life — an elevator operator caged, confined, desperate!

He relied on a $2,000 grant from the Canada Council to get him safely out of Canada. That's why he was the Canadian poet in residence when I discovered him in Hydra. Not that he needed discovery. He had already published a few books of poetry of varied quality.

It was a time when Canadian literature was struggling to express itself and be heard. It required a mix of independence, arrogance and governmental handout. Others, like Mordecai Richler, were struggling to create works that were not imitations of the angry young men of England or the rebels of Jewish American intellect like Philip Roth. But they somehow sounded too similar. In Mordecai's case, too angry to find the real richness of the roots which had provided him with life. He was truly promising. I recall strolling with him on a long London walk and telling him how I admired *Son of a Smaller Hero*. But the anger and European decadence would destroy any goodness that seemed to blossom. He seemed to me to become a garden of weeds — so little beauty in his splendid gift.

Leonard was luckier, more gentle, more decent. He needed to express his anger. He turned down the Canadian Governor-General's Award for Literature when offered. But so what? His poet's soul was intact.

He came close to the edge many times. But always, perhaps because of his solid tradition, pulled back in time. When he came to visit me at my garret penthouse in the New York village, he told me he had flirted with the idea of going to work at *TIME* magazine. *TIME* was a slow death for any real writer, except perhaps for James Agee. But like many thoroughbreds who have a natural charm, they also seem to have a charmed life.

In the sixties he would have an opportunity to sing a couple of his songs at the 92nd Street Y in New York, one of the great world platforms for poets — the place alcohol-soaked Dylan had come to pave the way.

His novel *Beautiful Losers* had become a Canadian success. The National Film Board of Canada found him and my skilled colleague Donald Brittain revealed what Leonard chose to reveal, a playful,

Photo: © Hazel Field

handsome devil in a bathtub, bather and poet, not yet singer.

He was lucky, too, in his timing. Then Sunday morning on television was still a time of experiment and discovery. WCBS in Manhattan still had a commercial free stage for talent. And so he sang his song on *Camera 3* with its stylized black and white splendor. No waste of money on sets or costumes. Make it if you can — just with talent. And so he did. And a helping hand of respect from Judy Collins proved a profitable assist. His program was the most popular in *Camera 3's* history.

And so he escaped the almost obscurity of the poet of the small press. Music, his music, would find him a worldwide audience.

Even *The New York Times* had to take notice. The eloquent music critic, John Rockwell, had to pay his reluctant compliments. Said, John Rockwell:

> there is a lot one could dislike about Leonard Cohen, the Canadian poet and songwriter... His voice is limited in range, his tunes sound repetitious and his persona is strange indeed — defensiveness elevated into art, with down right peculiar imagery and a constant, lugubrious pall over all.
> (But wait — here come the kisses and compliments)
> And yet he is pretty extraordinary, when all is said and done. The words are compulsive but they have the strength of genuine idiosyncratically imaginative verse. The tunes become hypnotic for their very repetitiousness, plaintive and modal in a manner that recalls medieval music and ancient folk tunes. Mr. Cohen's voice is limited in its range, it is quite evocative in color...
> Mr. Cohen seemed to emerge in the nineteen-sixties out of the post-Dylan American folk scene. But his way, even bitter sophistication, he really owes as much to chanting

Beat poets and the Continental Cabaret song as he does
to the folkier and blues revivalists...
The songs are full of varied imagery, but they keep
circling back to love. Not necessarily the simpler forms
of boy-girl love, although that is certainly central to his
concerns, but to older loves and spiritual loves as well.
The audience filled the hall and gave every sign of
helping that Mr. Cohen would return more frequently.

Leonard was truly the first great, vaginal poet. The women
adored, even lusted after the balladeer of their bodies. Leonard had
created a cult.

And I loved him for it, my Hydra pal, my brother. Who could
ignore him — I shared his new fame with delight. They heaped
their awkward praise on him, searching for comparisons, some so
remote as to be embarrassing. Leonard does that to people, you
know. He is so much himself he unnerves you.

Donald Henahan, the cultural editor of *The New York Times*
summarized him with:

On the alienation scale, he rates somewhere between
Schopenhauer and Bob Dylan, two other prominent
poets of pessimism. In capsule it might be said that
whereas Mr. Dylan is alienated from society and mad
about it, Mr. Cohen is alienated and merely sad about
it. Popular music is long overdue for a spell of neo-Keats
world-weariness and Mr. Cohen may well be its
spokesman this season.

It is simple to try and make Leonard and his appeal simple.
But the fact is he is as complex as a poem. What at first seems
obvious is of course not so. This is why he has survived while others
have and will vanish. He is, beneath it all, clear as he sings, "A singer

must die for the lie in his voice." And so the painter who strives for perfect colour and all artists who are constantly training to catch up with God, who will not be caught. But how wonderful to try!

The pop magazines tried to mold him in the mask of a pop hero. *People* magazine teased its readers with a photo of him in a gas mask and then half a dozen pages of romantic poses. The cut line announced, "The face may not be familiar, but the name should be — it's composer and cult hero Leonard Cohen." And the playful comment, "The worse my voice sounds, the more authentic." The writer of the article adds, "Laryngitis in London on his recent tour sent him to a throat specialist for vaporizing treatment."

And inside were portraits of the Cohen women. Leonard, my bachelor buddy, had married well, not exactly. He lived with a woman for nine years and had two children. I visited him in Montreal. She seemed out of context. Suzanne Elrod was a Miami Beach princess. The first name was correct, but all else, seemed wrong. Many a woman wept when they heard Leonard was gone. But it was just temporary. When they separated Leonard sadly mourned about her "Miami consumer habits." And then trying to set it all right he declared, "My only luxuries are airplane tickets to go anywhere at any time. All I need is a table, chair and bed."

He sat down and made out his own agreement of separation. Leonard was back but damaged, but perhaps enriched. He hurt because his "marriage" was a mess. But the father role was something that appealed to his deep patriarchal Cohen roots. He could not escape his Old Testament beliefs. Nor did he want to.

I list all this by way of introduction. And it might have seemed obvious and certain that we would link up to create a film. I liked him and enjoyed him. It was mutual. I did not share with the critics their belief in his essential gloom. I found his constant belief in love appealing. And his spiritual awareness made me always feel at home beside him.

I had been making films about some of the truly great creative spirits of our century, such as playwright Tennessee Williams and painter Marc Chagall. Why not my pal Leonard Cohen?

I had had a rather terrifying experience previously in filmmaking with another singer — Bob Dylan. It now came time to attempt a film on Leonard. Could I handle it? I could not approach it lightly or without fear. There was a major difference — I knew Leonard, we had been on a quest together in our young years. And this would be a film about a singer of songs about love, not relentless anger. I was sure of his personal quality, his faith, his tradition and his personal integrity.

Sure, Leonard had had his time of rejecting the system, finding its basic faults, buy also the intelligence to compare my theologies.

He was an early fellow traveler to Cuba. He had gone to Cuba to support Castro, during the Bay of Pigs. But then the adventure turned into a communist mess. He was arrested when he decided to leave, but somehow managed to escape his guard and get on a plane, bound for Miami.

I found myself when I made *Cuba and Castro Today* that it was a no-win place, with a no-win system. Everything seemed so simple when I was touring the island with the maximum leader, but then when he was out of range, the machine guns were turned on me. Kafka would understand.

As in most of Leonard's adventures, not all positive, out would emerge a poem-song:

Parachuting Acid into diplomatic cocktail parties
Urging Fidel Castro to abandon fields and castles
Leave it all like a man
Come back to nothing special
And silver bullet suicides
And Messianic ocean tides
And racial roller coaster rides
And other forms of boredom advertised
as poetry.

I know you need your sleep now,
And I know you life's been hard
But many men are falling where you
promised to stand guard.

I never asked, but I heard that you cast
your lot along with the poor
How come I overheard your prayer that
You be this and nothing more
Than just some grateful, faithful
Woman favorite singing millionaire
The patron Saint of envy and the
Grocer of despair
Working for the Yankee Dollar.

I like what critic Paul Nelson wrote twenty-five years ago in *Rolling Stone* about the early, but always evolving, Cohen — always true to himself no matter what the price:

> His solitude, which he seems to carry with him everywhere — even on stage — was, in a way far more moving than the audience's enthusiastic acceptance of his work. The Russian poet Joseph Brodsky has written: "Alas, unless a man can manage to eclipse the world, he's left to twirl a gap-toothed dial in some phone booth,

Photo: © Hazel Field

as one night spin a Ouija board, until a phantom answers, echoing the last words of a buzzer in the night.

Leonard Cohen may be that phantom.

How to capture the phantom? With my film crew I studied all the films made about singers on tour, including a recent one by the noted director Martin Scorcese. I found their strengths and then their many faults. To make this film was like planning a battle. I required total cooperation — the music, the men had to be on cue.

The day would come when I would meet with Leonard to make the proposal. It was a complex rendezvous. We planned a dinner at Toronto's Courtyard Café in the Windsor Arms Hotel. We exchanged our fears about trying to find the phantom.

In my case I had also just had an X-ray for a stomach ulcer. And perhaps it was all those Dylan memories coming back to haunt me. The X-ray showed a vast dark shadow, causing panic in my heart. I told Leonard I was determined to go ahead with the project even if I was dying.

Leonard, as always, was considerate and consoling and offered, "Harry that's not the problem, you are not going to die."

As we leaned forward, two sad-eyed Jews at the Courtyard Café, two young women intruded. "Mr. Cohen we just love you to death — love your music. Is it really you? I can't believe it, wait till I tell everyone."

I suggest, as politely as possible, to the eager moist female to back off, as I was sure I was dying." She snapped at me, "So, what does that have to do with me?"

And then, abruptly changing her tone coyly to Leonard, "Oh, just one picture together, Leonard. This is so exciting."

I was left to die a little in the corner till this always-necessary homage was completed — a ritual I would see repeated many times in many places. And the shy, sad eyed Leonard, was as always polite.

As they giggled away, across the crowded room, Leonard returned to the interrupted conversation.

"If you really want to do a film about a man who is really probably finished, we can try." We decided to try.

Leonard was feeling the unimaginable grief of his separation. He did not want to be a part-time father. He was blaming himself, made no comments about his gypsy wife. Not then. But he would tell the tale in many ways in poems and song.

It seemed to me that one of the problems I would confront is the easy fix — attempt to find the simple way to analyze the icon Leonard had become, from obscure poet on a Greek Island to the sensitive, singing soul whose fans wanted to touch and to whom many world leaders felt they had some special kinship. He was said to have become the favorite singer of two French presidents. A German critic of note pronounced, "he is the incarnation of the unfulfilled wishes and unanswered questions of the young generation."

A Toronto critic, William French, declared after an interview, "Yet, this day, he still looks forlorn and vulnerable, possessor of a secret sad wisdom denied the rest of us. That's one reason why women are attracted to him, that knowledge of hidden places and secret delights."

Maybe, perhaps. I decided from the start that the film I made would have no commentary, no third person narrative. It would unfold like a song itself, like a concert for the emotion. First would come the ingathering of conversation, published here as it happened, starting with an extensive interview in Montreal. He had then set the center of his life, his roots, in a place where he had had no physical roots, in an apartment just east of "The Main", St. Lawrence Boulevard, his own solitude between the two solitudes of French and English Montreal. Once it was Jewish, but now it has a mixture of immigrants.

In the past, the irony of his physical setting was not lost on

Leonard. Mordecai Richler grew up around the corner and then fought to find his way into the sun of Westmount, the affluent middle-class suburb in the city. And Leonard, born to the privilege of Westmont, found a kind of tranquility in the cramped dwellings of his adopted home. Here he was striving, as always "to be free."

The apartment itself had the stark whiteness of Hydra. You felt almost as if a whitewash brush had parched it before I arrived. A cool breeze made the white lace curtains dance in and out to their own music. And so, at Leonard's substantial writing table we began, a shaky start. My fault.

But I turn to the transcript, as I have kept it for twenty years, even when it is a little personally embarrassing.

"Well, what is the most important thing to you?"

"That is a terrible question."

"To feel you have communicated a notion? To feel you have lived a good life? I am suggesting all kinds of things, okay!" And so the pompous question elicited the predictable put-on answer. Shades of Bob Dylan, when would I ever learn? If anything, looking back in time, at that time, Leonard was most polite in his response to a gauche interviewer.

"It is a hell of a question for Monday morning," Leonard answered with some tolerance. "I feel in a way the most important thing is to get to the Y, four or five times a week. I am really not trying to be facetious, but I think that out of that kind of sense of well-being a proper perspective is established. And, that is what I would like to do."

I tried to play the game, even if I was not sure then what the game was.

"Okay, so you are saying what is very important is why you are alive. To have a body that is functioning, to take along whatever else is going on, correct? Yeah?"

This elicited a one-word answer.

"Yeah."

Try again.

"So that you are totally involved in the universe around you in a kind of way, physical, mental, right?"

Leonard looked sadly at me, wondering, I think, what he had gotten into.

"So you are not totally involved in your own disease."

"You better explain that." I said.

"Well there are certain kinds of thoughts that accompany that kind of position, this kind of posture and you know after swimming a quarter of a mile, you feel very different about things."

(As a swimmer, I did understand, but tried to bring the conversation to a more manageable place.)

"Okay, I get that. How about in terms of human relationships. You have had your ups and downs, and difficulties in a way it seems to me your new album is a reflection of almost — it seems to me hearing it — you feel it is almost, as if you sound emancipated. I do not know if that is true or not, unchained."

Half-smile was my reward. "That's pretty good. I do."

I was struggling.

"But does that make you feel more — let me try it again — is it important to love the whole world or one person?"

This let loose a flow of ideas that continued for many weeks of filming. He started with a denial.

"I can't see this...I can't see those as...oh I don't even know how to say it. I mean they are not mutually exclusive — I don't, I don't have those constellations of thought, of one person or the whole world or what is necessary to do, or you feel. I don't... that sounds like a program. I think there are writers who have that kind of ideological program. Some good writers, probably have that kind of ideological program and a lot of very poor writers and that's the kind that is when you become your own commissar and you establish for yourself what is the proper motive or mode of expression. And, the faculties of censorship are working overtime.

That has never been my way of doing it. And, I don't know. Irving Layton said a kind thing about me once, he said, something like my mind has never been contaminated by a single idea. I don't really have many ideas about things or the way things should be."

"Okay. Irving Layton has been important to you." Leonard seemed much more comfortable with the change of subject.

"He is a close friend of mine. And you know he's important as a figure, as a spirit in this country. Beyond my friendship with him, I recognize what he is, in this country, which is an unfailing spring of vitality. As a friend of course, you stop seeing people in those kind of grand terms and just enjoy the nourishment of the friendship."

But I wanted to return to the idea of ideas. "But the thing he said about you, in terms of not having an idea of something, does that mean that — do you think — that maybe you are just more involved with the fragment of emotions, of things, and that it is hard to put into words. That your preoccupation is with the details of emotion?"

Leonard responded in a way that I then found confusing.

"I don't feel I have a preoccupation. I probably do have one but I don't seem to operate out of a sense of preoccupation. As you get older, your life becomes established in certain realms and your work becomes clearer and the challenges of the work itself determine much of your activity. In other words, I know that I want to write songs. I can't examine why I want to write songs, or what made me want to write songs. I could offer all kinds of constructions but, once you know that is what you are doing, you apply yourself to that work with an energy that you will have to, of which you have to be a good custodian and a memory of the techniques and devices of the craft. But most of all the rigorous resources to keep these available, they become the nature of the work. In other words you don't want to get yourself into a kind of condition where you can't draw on your experience."

I switched gear again.

"In the summer you go off to this retreat, why do you do that?"

"I have done that for a couple of summers, I tend to find that if you are going to take a month or two off, every year or even a week...and I don't know why I do it."

"Well I suppose what I am trying to find out is - is it because you find it difficult to find a peace of mind in everyday activity that you have got to lock yourself off to find that peace of mind, or is that a lack of understanding on my part to ask the question?"

"I don't know, it might be, but it's not really. The goal is not really peace of mind."

I had much to learn about the ways of my friend. "The goal is?"

"Well I am not too sure what the goal is, for writing a poem, or sitting by yourself somewhere, but I don't think it is peace of mind. I think it's a much more rigorous activity. It's more like housecleaning than meditation. By meditation we somehow mean someone sitting alone with God, but those moments that I have had in that kind of activity — I don't mean formal meditation, but just going off somewhere, they are — the activity is rigorous."

"Help me to understand," I almost pleaded.

"I just meant...I just said that to toss off the conventional vision of what a retreat is. Or what the conditions, what are the conditions that prevail when someone takes a week or two off and tries to establish another foundation for themselves."

"Well is God in your head, something like the old man you would have studied with the beard and the bible of your childhood?"

He tried to end the questioning of this kind.

"Sometimes," he said.

"And sometimes?" I insisted.

He let me have it, as it were.

"Sometimes not. Speaking of God, of course, is our right and the privilege to speak to God in an objective sense. You know God and to satisfy your appetites for worship and for obedience those are all the legitimate appetites of the human nature but they come out of the subject/object world. In other words we are here, and the God as we determine the God to be, is over there and that is our ordinary perception of the system and it's also legitimate. But there are other conditions in which we don't have that subject/object relationship. It dissolves and we experience ourselves as the content of everything that arises. And, some people call that God. It is just another kind of experience in which there is no subject and object. But in ordinary conversation and in ordinary ceremonial activity which we also have an appetite for, the objective God is a satisfactory device, to satisfy many human appetites."

I didn't know what to say. I felt like Jacob wrestling with the angels. I offered to surrender. "All right, it is all right with me."

Pardon.

[Out of film.]

And just in time – because it was a bad start. Let us try again.

Not one word of the above made it into the film. It was too early to begin to find God. Slowly, slowly and, indeed, that question is crucial to *The Song of Leonard Cohen*.

Taking a more down-to-earth, sensible approach... we moved to a back balcony of his second floor apartment.

"Who lives around here?" I asked, relieved to be elsewhere in location and thought.

"Hazel lives over there."

Leonard playfully gestured to the next balcony.

"Hazel, get up." He hollered to a closed window.

I wanted to know more about the neighborhood.

"And how about below you, who lives below?

"Mr. and Mrs. Deluca. And their daughter Angela."

Leonard relished his knowledge of the folks around.

"There is a Polish lady who lives in that balcony. She comes out every morning at about six. Until last year there was a shed here, she used to chop her own wood every morning."

"Well some people might look out and say, 'why do you want to live over all these shacks and old balconies?'"

One again he toyed with me. But maybe not.

"Not very many people." The sun just came out.

Leonard took a portable radio with his new recording tape in it and I asked if he would play it.

"Yeah, the beginning of this is kind of louder than the middle part, so I will just hold the volume down a bit.

He recited the lyrics to the French words...

> *There was a wandering Canadian*
> *Banished from his home and heart*
> *He wandered around weeping*
> *Through foreign countries and lands*
> *One day sad and lonely*
> *Seated beside a river*
> *To the meandering stream,*
> *He said these words,*
> *If you see my country,*
> *And if you get to my county*
> *My most unfortunate country,*
> *Go and speak to all my friends*
> *Tell them that I remember them.*

And then to Hazel who climbed out her window to join us. It was a left bank moment. Hazel Field was a young photographer and a Leonard admirer.

"I will have that coffee Hazel, come climb up and give it to me."

"It's very instrumental. Here —"

"Thanks a lot Hazie, come on over and bring Alfie."

Hazel made an entrance with Alfie her dog.

"Do you feel like the person in that song, *A Canadian Wandering*

Around...Do you think?"
"A little bit."

Oh days so full of trial
You have disappeared
And my country alas
I will never see it again

"Why a French Canadian song?" I wanted to know.

It would eventually make a marvelous start for my film.

Leonard, the constant searcher, far from home, even when he was home. That vague dimension — everywhere and nowhere — the same place. Then came one of those marvelous documentary moments — the crew must always be prepared for them. They add reality and immediacy. Irving Layton, the boyish mentor of Cohen, an early verbal-poet, knocked on the door and shouted up from below, with an attractive blonde beside him. Leonard was holding court. Layton in striped bright costume called up from the street.

"Leonard, are you in? Open the door. How long do you want me to keep on knocking at the door, what are you doing anyway?"

Layton, professional poet and extrovert, had arrived. A key was tossed down and Irving arrived and the party of poets began. It was a marvel to behold, the two generations enjoying each other — a treasure of pleasure. Irving more than made up for Leonard's basic shyness. Leonard explained his hyper friend.

"Irving is always the same way."

I suggested they carry on as if the film crew had vanished and they did.

"I think it is interesting to hear you talk about what you have both been doing. Together.

(And so they improvised a conversation that became a scene in the film.)

Leonard is not too great at small talk.

"What have you been doing Irving?"

Irving always seemed to be on stage to the world.

"What am I ever doing? Getting into trouble. I go about, what are some of the immortal lines of mine, I go around making trouble for myself, the sparks fly, I gather each one and start a poem. And I gather you do the same thing. In your own way, in your own inevitable way. You do the same thing, you just make trouble for yourself."

Leonard was amused by his comrade of words.

"Yeah, Irving, you know you always used to say to me. Leonard are you sure you are doing the wrong thing?"

"Yes. My favorite saying. Leonard, are you sure you are doing the wrong thing? Yes. You have grown more certain with the years, right?"

Leonard was curious about a recent geographical change in his friend's life.

"Right, I want to ask you about this move to Niagara? How do you find it out there?"

Irving quickly waxed rhapsodic. "Sounds sinister, but it's great."

"It's great?"

Left to right: Irving Layton, Sandra, Leonard Cohen, Hazel Field

Left to right: Harry Rasky, Irving Layton, Sandra, Leonard Cohen,

"Beautiful."

"...out there?"

"It's full of orchards, vineyards and WASPs. Marvelous combination really. In fact I have already written my first anti-Niagara-on-the-Lake poem and it's called *A Perfect Man*. There is a place called The Buttery, the name itself tells you everything you want to know, but it's where white-haired, pink-cheeked WASP biddies come for their tea and crumpets and it's a kind of grotesque, funny analog to the Mediterranean outdoor café. Because you know in Rome or Milan or any of the Italian cities, you have people drinking wine and conversing with great animation as a rule. Picture to yourself these white-haired, pink faced, apple-cheeked WASP biddies having tea and crumpets, not raising their voice ever above the level of a whisper and every now and then a clerical figure appearing to make sure that decorum is kept at all times as they..."

Cohen and Layton liked to have verbal play – master and student. Leonard smiled. "Sounds like the kind of place I would like."

Irving was prepared to play the host. "You are welcome to

come, so I have written my first tirade poem against Niagara-on-the-Lake and it is a beginning of course of a whole..."

Leonard interrupts with a somewhat mocking, "It sounds peaceful."

Layton was fond of the art of bluster.

"It won't be long after my poetry is read, my poems are read, what I'm hoping you know why I am doing it, look... you can do it too, why not, you are a good friend, you're a good Jewish boy you want to make a dollar, I'll tell you how to do it. I bought a house, right. And I sat publishing my poems and reciting my poems and they are really vicious, savage poems that I am writing. So eventually within about six months they will come and they will offer me three times the amount to just move out you know."

"That's a good way to make money." Leonard encouraged his friend's wild fantasy. "And then you will go to Stratford and work the same scam."

"Right, I was thinking that about a lot of towns in Ontario."

The talk encouraged a painful pun.

"...like Niagara-on-the-Lake they are changing to Niagar- on-the-Layton, so then you can go to Stratford."

Irving of course tried to point out his protest. "I can think of more pleasant things on Layton than Niagara, can't you?"

"Anyway the poem, if you are interested, imagines...me imagining the true resurrection story. If only the resurrection story were true. And you and I could get together at The Buttery. To talk about the perfect erection you showed James and Judas while the white-haired, apple-cheeked ladies and the local minister, at the other tables were straining their necks to overhear our conversation. See, Niagara-on-the-Lake, I conclude will never be the same, right?"

Leonard offered some verbal applause.

"Right."

Irving was determined to continue while he had center stage.

"So that is my fantasy. Among other fantasies...you have them all the time when you walk there. It's a good idea to go there. Well the contract is so overwhelming, Leonard, that all kinds of strange ideas you know, like I have a theory. I don't know whether I ever told you this theory. I have a theory that what people call senility... see I have a sister who is senile, and that is why you know my poem *Senile My Sister Sings*... ah it's a poem that you can't live without. It's in my forthcoming book, it's one of the great, great poems."

Always respectfully humoring his senior friend, Leonard played straight-man, as it were.

"I have heard..."

And so Irving acted on.

"After this poem, Shakespeare, Chaucer, forget them. It's one of the great poems of the English language. You know, I am modest but I can tell these things. Well, my sister sings, she does nothing else. When you see her...like my brother Harry traveled all the way from California to see her and she greeted him the same way, she just didn't recognize him. She just sang and when I went to see her, she sang. And I have been thinking about why does my sister sing all the time. And it occurred to me that the real explanation for senility is not the traditional one that it's a failure of oxygen to the brain cells. It is in senility that we take on the personality that we repress all our lives. How my sister wanted to be a singer! She had a magnificent voice and if she had the parents with the money, as well as the discernment, she could have become one of the great, great sopranos. So that is why she sings, because the real Esther that never had a chance, to blossom, to thrive in this world, is coming out."

Leonard poured the potion for poetry.

"Any wine here?"

And so a ritual was enacted. After the teacher had an opportunity to show off, the new star would show his works.

"Aspirin or whatever. Where is our wine girl?"

"No, we don't want that. Don't say 'wine girl.'"

Leonard didn't like the chauvinistic reference to Hazel who served more wine.

Irving was cautioned.

"Is it wine from our own country?"

"That's right, I'm a nationalist. A patriot."

Irving sampled the new bottle with a semi-grimace.

"Well, that's not champagne."

"Where is your glass, Hazel?"

Leonard poured one of several glasses of wine, the poets on parade.

Now was the moment.

"Want to hear a song, Irv?"

"Leonard, I would like to hear some of your new songs. Are you going to play them for me."

He brought his portable player and played his new recording.

"I've got one right here."

"It looks as though you've got several. Start at the beginning."

"This is one song, Irving."

"What, you're not going to let me hear any more than one song?"

The mood changed with the music. It was obvious that Layton now was marveling at skills he admired and perhaps envied. The poet was a also composer. Now you could hear the glory of poems and music combined.

"That's beautiful, that is really very beautiful."

The melody filled the room. Irving was actually stunned. He was in awe.

"That is the most beautiful thing you have ever written."

The silent blonde offered her one comment to the pair of poets.

"Very beautiful."

I then decided to turn the questioning to the teacher, to Layton. I asked Irving, who seemed really to express views easily: "I have to ask you a question. It is a nice warm, Montreal day, for people from other parts of the world and the other parts of Canada. Why do you think that the outstanding writers of a certain time have come from Montreal and I think of poetic spirits like Leonard Cohen, the subject of this film, Mordecai Richler, the poet A.M. Klein and Irving Layton, what was it that made that happen? Now that we have you here on the spot, I would be very interested."

Irving was pleased to play the stage. He said, with an easy smile. "Personally I can't refrain from pointing out that the four writers that you have mentioned are all Jewish and that's a significant factor and it bears on the answer that I want to give. What you had in Montreal was a Jewish community that was very cohesive, the sort of thing that you don't have in Toronto. Not only cohesive but also very self aware, very self-conscious. You have a Jewish community in Toronto, you had and have Jewish communities in Winnipeg and Regina and so on. They may have the same cohesiveness but not he same self-awareness. We came out of a Jewish life or a Jewish milieu that was cohesive, dynamic, and also self-aware. But there had to be one additional factor. There had to be three solitudes, which is what existed in Montreal. You had three ghettoes, you had three peoples, the Anglos, the French Canadians and the Jews and they peered at each other over these walls. The Jews, you know, having always had the gift of anxiety, were more aware of the French Canadians and the English Canadians, than let us say the Italians or the Portuguese, who are also in minority. But Jews, with their long tradition of persecution, of anguish, of pain, have become peculiarly sensitized. Now out of that sensitivity and pain and anguish and solitude have come the writers Mordecai Richler, A.M. Klein, Leonard Cohen and myself. We have also had Henry Moscovitch, and a Seymour Mayne and so on. So, that is the explanation."

Since Layton was in a professional mood, I asked him to go deeper in his analysis. "But the themes that they are writing about are not necessarily Jewish themes and the writings that have universal and international appeal, why is that?"

Irving stretched himself out, swallowed another glass of afternoon wine, and explained.

"Ah, but again the answer is that they don't have to be Jewish, specifically Jewish. What you have is that gift of anxiety and pain and alienation and solitude, which has become very contemporary. It has become universal. In fact, the whole world has become Jewish. You know in view of the fact that we are all menaced with extinction. Once upon a time the Jew held that he, particularly, was menaced, that there would be a *pogrom*, there would be a holocaust, as indeed, there was a holocaust. But in other words, his life was in danger. Today, everybody is caught up with the Jew, everybody's life is in danger, right? With that, you know the chances of a nuclear holocaust are increasing, so nobody feels secure. Nobody feels happy. That is Jewish. When you don't feel secure and happy, that is being Jewish. For this reason, all these writers have expressed the alienation, the pain, the anguish, and the fear, which everybody feels today."

I wanted the focus back on Leonard who was sitting contently, enjoying his old teacher.

I prodded Layton: "Okay, you were kind of an early mentor of Leonard's. What was it that you saw in him, his early work, that turned you on and made you feel that this was a voice that was an important voice."

Layton was anxious to argue as usual: "Correction, I was never a mentor."

"Okay." I wanted to keep the dialogue going — Layton followed through, as if an old Jew discussing the Talmud.

"Correction, I have to correct that. Leonard was a genius from the first moment I saw him. I have nothing to teach him. I have doors to open which I did. I opened doors for all the younger writers. Possibly the doors would have been opened by Leonard himself. But the fact is simply because I was older, I opened the doors of sexual expression, of freedom of expression and so on and so forth. Once the doors were opened, Leonard marched very confidently along a path, a path and a road somewhat different from my own. But I was never his mentor. I wish I could claim that I was his mentor, but I cannot claim that. That honor does not belong to me, only to God."

Layton relished the comparison. He delighted in the comparison.

I had to ask: "Do you wish sometimes... that maybe you had put your own poems to music. It seems to be a way of just carrying poems beyond the boundary. The boundaries seem to keep poets in a certain spot. Whereas the addition of music seems to allow them to expand to new horizons."

Layton mused about the muse and necessity.

"Well Leonard was perceptive enough, I think, to see fifteen or twenty years ago that something was happening to poetry and he didn't want to have his poems fingered by academics and he didn't want to have the new critics working on his poems to find the erudite meanings in them, you know. He had the good sense and the wisdom to see that there is a big audience out there that would be reached by music and by ballads. In other words, he, I think, saw that he had to be someone quite different from the kind of academic, scholarly poets like A.J.M. Smith or Louis Dudek or F.R. Scott, that he had to be a balladeer, a modern balladeer. There are for me many similarities, between Leonard's ballads, Leonard's songs and the ballads written in the twelfth and thirteenth century. The quality of mystery, of doom, of menace, of sadness, the dramatic quality that you will find in the Scottish ballads, in the English ballads of the thirteenth century — I find the same quality in Leonard Cohen's work."

It was a rich Montreal afternoon for poems and ideas.

I asked, "Do you find his songs sad, or do you find joy in them?"

Layton was exceedingly generous. He loved praising his

protégé. "There is both. What I like particularly in Leonard's songs is what I call their manic-depressive or rather the depressive-manic quality to be quite accurate. If you notice in some of his most telling and most moving songs, they always begin on a note of pain, of anguish, of sadness and then somehow or other he works himself up into a state of exaltation, of euphoria as if he had released himself from the devils of melancholy and of pain. These for me are Leonard's most typical and most powerful songs, like the first one which is reminiscent of another one of his. Suddenly you know, after groaning and moaning and pain and anguish, all very moving, and all very telling, suddenly there is an upbeat, a very euphoric, outburst of joy and it is a joy that is earned, because he has paid the price of suffering and in pain and insight. So for me, Leonard is a very significant troubadour of our time because we all pay the price of anguish and frustration and unhappiness. And Leonard pays that price. But he has the insistence on not allowing himself to be trapped forever or crippled in that mood. In other words, for me he is a heroic troubadour. For me he is a tragic, heroic troubadour and that is what I find most appealing in Leonard's work. It always moves me. It never fails to move me very deeply because it is the heroism of our time where we cannot call on God, or destiny or communism or socialism or nationalism to help us. It is the man alone, alienated, by himself. He has to work out his own salvation. Leonard works out a salvation musically. See...and he does it with great genius."

I turned to Leonard who took it all in with the wine of the day.

"Do you accept that Leonard?"

With a sly smile, he nodded his approval and said: "I accept it."

We all laughed and filled our glasses. There was still more to be said.

"Okay, just to pursue this a little bit further, very eloquent, very beautiful. These Jewish Canadian writers, are they different than the American Jewish writers. You know, we are talking about

Bellow and Roth and all those characters that came up after the war. How do they differ?"

Layton was quick with his analysis.

"The difference is first of all, they are more assimilationist than the Jewish writers in Canada because they don't have the community that stood behind Leonard and myself and Mordecai and Klein. The Jewish milieu there is a much more unstable community than the one that existed up until now, in Montreal. Like Leonard comes out of a very old, very renowned patrician Jewish family. Now that gives a kind of strength and self-confidence. I come out of a very pious orthodox Jewish life which again gave me a confidence and a strength and the same thing goes for A.M. Klein. That does not exist in the United States and therefore, the Jewish note is of a different kind. Either it is extremely self-critical, in the work of Roth, almost nasty, you know, kind of self-hatred even, which you don't find in Canada. You have it a little bit in Mordecai Richler, but it is compensated for by his very rich and broad humor and his wit and so on."

The conversation was so intense. We all almost forgot about the presence of the crew. We ran out of film and I tried to return to the thought while the camera was being readied.

"So you were talking about the difference. I think it is very important to pick it up again because we ran out of film. But the difference between this group of Canadian Jewish writers, largely emanating from Montreal and the American equivalent that received so much attention, carrying such persons as Saul Bellow all the way up to the Nobel Prize. What is the difference again?"

Layton had no trouble catching his breath and the idea. He was not a man short of words.

"Well, for me the difference is that you don't have, you haven't had the assimilationist tendencies in Montreal or for that matter in Toronto, that you had in the United States. Saul Bellow or say Norman Mailer, or Roth, I don't think they had the kind of background and the kind of psychological security that the Jewish writers in Montreal had. The Jewish writers in Montreal did not have to turn their backs on their Jewish background, on their Jewish milieu. They could appropriate whatever they felt was important to their own work and make a significant blend between their Jewishness and their Canadian environment. They didn't have to revolt against their Jewish background, hate it or despise it or satirize it mercilessly. They never felt inferior to the English Canadians or the French Canadians. Sometimes they had the problem of restraining their sense of superiority but that's a different kind of thing entirely, you see. Whereas, my feeling, is that the American Jewish writer was made to feel, right from the start, that he was a strange animal, a different sort of animal, inferior, he had to watch his manners. To begin with he had to watch his accent. In other words ever-watchful, ever-suspicious of his origins. Now that does not create that kind of confidence out of which comes the robust poetry or the songs or the ballads the Jew could hear in Montreal where he could make use of his gift of anxiety and above all his great gift of historical indignation, without feeling that he is inferior. It's like those Jews who, in a gentile environment if they became excited, and they begin to gesticulate which is their natural way of talking, would have to watch themselves because you're not supposed to do that, certainly not down in Maryland, or North Carolina, or in the better suburbs of New York. You watch this excitability because that marks you as Jewish. The point is that here the Jewish writer could live with his excitability. He could draw on his excitability. He could develop his tantrum and he could blend that temperament and with the English Canadian, the WASP, or the French Canadian. He could go on assimilating rather than being assimilated. I have drawn on Catholicism. I have drawn on Protestantism. I have criticized satirized Protestantism or Catholicism. So with us it was a different thing entirely. We could assimilate what they had to give us without being destroyed in the process."

Leonard was different from the rest from the start. I suggested, "In Leonard's case, coming from a Westmont home — some people may find that a peculiar beginning for a poet. Usually they think of a poet coming out of the sad soil of the place or something like that. How do you think that affected him since he's siting right next to you?"

Another laugh from all.

"Well, Leonard was a genius, he was able to find the sadness in Westmont. You know that takes genius. He was able to see that not all rich people, not all comfortable people, not all Plutocrats were happy. That was a myth you see. If you had money, and that was certainly the American myth, if you were well off, if you had a house in Westmount, and certainly if you had a house in upper Westmont, then you were blessed, you had everything. Now Leonard had the insight, the genius, to realize that this is not necessarily so. Now what is genius? Genius is the ability — it's a very rare ability — to see things as they actually are. You are not fooled. That to me is the strictest definition of genius that I know. A genius is someone who sees things exactly as they are. And, there is no law about that, a genius can be born in a hovel. He can be born in a slum and can be born in Westmount. So, Leonard was born in Westmount. He took a look and he saw that there were just as many frustrated, unhappy miserable souls in Westmount, as there are happy people in the neighborhood where he is now living, in St. Urbain."

That ended our search for the source of inspiration, or perhaps genius, for the day. I asked Irving, "Do you have a favorite Leonard Cohen poem?"

Layton was happy to please. "I have many, many favorites."

I asked, "Are there any in this book?" I passed him a copy of the then newly published *Death of a Lady's Man*, which I considered a great, provocative title.

Irving responded, "In here, yes, there is the title poem."

I anxiously requested, "Would you read it? I think that would be kind of interesting, to have you reading one of Leonard's poems."

Layton, poet, now became performer, a role he enjoyed: "The title poem. Yeah, that lovely ballad.

This is the title poem, *Death of Lady's Man:*

The man she wanted all her life
*   was hanging by a thread.*
"I never even knew how much
*   I wanted you," she said.*
His muscles they were numbered
*   and his style was obsolete.*
"O baby, I have come too late."
*   She knelt beside his feet.*

"I'll never see a face like yours
*   in years of men to come,*
I'll never see such arms again
*   in wrestling or in love."*
And all his virtues burning
*   in this smoky holocaust,*
she took unto herself
*   most everything her lover lost.*

Now the master of this landscape
*   he was standing at the view*
with a sparrow of St. Francis
*   that he was preaching to.*
She beckoned to the sentry
*   of his high religious mood.*
She said, "I'll make a space between my legs,
*   I'll teach you solitude."*

He offered her an orgy
    in a many-mirrored room;
he promised her protection
    for the issue of her womb.
She moved her body hard
    against a sharpened metal spoon,
she stopped the bloody rituals
    of passage to the moon.

She took his much-admired
    oriental frame of mind,
and the heart-of-darkness alibi
    his money hides behind.
She took his blonde madonna
    and his monastery wine.
"This mental space is occupied
    and everything is mine."

He tried to make a final stand
    beside the railway track.
She said, "The art of longing's over
    and it's never coming back."
She took his tavern parliament,
    his cap, his cocky dance;
she mocked his female fashions
    and his working-class moustache.

The last time that I saw him
    he was trying hard to get
a woman's education
    but he's not a woman yet.
And the last time that I saw her
    she was living with a boy

who gives her soul an empty room
    and gives her body joy.

So the great affair is over
    but whoever would have guessed
it would leave us all so vacant
    and so deeply unimpressed.
It's like our visit to the moon
    or to that other star:
I guess you go for nothing
    if you really want to go that far.

"Bravo," I said and meant it. Layton, with his silvery, wavy hair and matinee idol style had given a younger poet an older poet's passion.

Leonard said, "It's a great honor to hear you read that."

And Layton responded with relish, almost tasting the delight of the words: "It's a beautiful poem, it's a beautiful poem. It's a great honor to read it. He has many great wonderful poems, I talked about Leonard a year ago when I was at York University, at a graduate seminar, of Montreal poets and Leonard was of course one of the poets. It was always a great lift to come to Leonard's poetry after say F.R. Scott or Louis Dudek and others. There is a signature to his poetry."

I wanted to know if that formative time had passed.

"But is it over," Leonard was saying. "Maybe it is all over for this group that has come up from Montreal. This tradition?"

Layton responded: "Yes I think it is, because the milieu is cracking. They, the three solitudes, have become one big solitude you see and you don't have the tensions anymore out of which the Jewish writers came and their French Canadian writers are riding a tide of nationalism which is a different thing entirely and therefore I don't think they have a universal voice. Because the universal voice, I regret to say, is not one of buoyancy and aggressiveness, but one of doubt and of uncertainty and the Jews have given expression to that mood of doubt and uncertainty. The old sign posts are down, Leonard's songs dealing with the difficulties between male and female in a modern setting. There have always been difficulties between male and female. But in a modern setting where women are challenging as men have never been challenged before, where the family as an institution appears to be crumbling and various pressures, of one kind or another, that are breaking in on people. Well Leonard's songs are expressing the predicaments we find ourselves in."

"Stop there," I said and the filming was over for the afternoon. We knew we had been part of an important moment. I was honoured to have been allowed in. It had its own rhythm and vitality, like a poem itself.

We all have moments and people in our lives of varying significance. We tend to favor a time of growing emotion of emotional pain. The next filming session was with one of these individuals. A pal, the sculptor Mort Rosengarten, who had grown up on Leonard's Westmount street and then shared a room in college. Together, we entered Cookie's restaurant and a ritual was being enacted.

"Good morning, Mr. Solomon. How are you?" Leonard greeted the owner of the humble coffee shop.

Mr. Solomon, in his apron and flashing front gold tooth responded. "Good, you?" Leonard and Mort lapsed into, small talk.

Mort, as subdued as Layton is gregarious, said: "I took a walk in the cemetery the other day. Something that I have been planning to do for years."

"Which one?"

"The big Catholic cemetery. My friend kept remarking on the

size of North American angel wings and how large they are."

"I think she is an angel."

"I did ask her where hers were."

"I always thought that the angels in the cemetery were made in Italy."

"Where are they made?"

"Heaven."

"I went up to do some repair. I was out with Cherie and I said I would like to really visit a cemetery this was about 2:00 in the morning and I said, 'The only one within walking distance is ... and I think the gates are closed at night.'

She said, 'Well maybe we could climb over the gate.'

I said, 'I don't think it's appropriate. Climb over a gate, get caught climbing over the gate into the cemetery. Anyhow curiously enough the gates were open and there was a car parked there and there was something going on so we walked in and we visited my mother's grave and it was very nice.'"

"She wasn't there."

I decided to divert the conversation, "How long have you and Mort been friends. How far back does it go?"

Leonard decided to divert me: "I think it was a Wednesday we met. I guess we have been friends for about thirty-five years."

I asked, "Do you correspond, I mean, because Leonard, you are away so often?"

Since Leonard and I have been friends I could have predicted the response. Although he did ask if I have an e-mail address, which I cannot use.

"I have received one post card, I think it was in 1963."

Mort, more serious, "Let's see, him I sent him a postcard once, it was in bronze, it was when... and I did this card in bronze and all the lettering was... mailed it off to Greece and he never got it. His address at that time was just Cohen...Greece."

Leonard seemed playfully surprised.

"I never did get that, never heard of it again."

"I am pretty sure I mailed it. I may never have mailed it."

"You probably just put a stamp on it and dropped it in the mail box."

I asked Mort about a character like him in *Beautiful Losers*.

"How do you feel about having appeared as a fictitious character in a book Mort? In one of Leonard's early books?"

"I had fun reading the book," he said.

Leonard said, "It was not really accurate from the point of view of actual events, just the context, the context was authentic. But the actual character that Rosencrantz had in the book, is not at all like Rosengarten's character."

As someone born in a lower income area, I had difficulty with the downgrading of living area.

"Mort, you are also a product of Westmount. You moved down

Photo: © Hazel Field

Left to right, Mort Rosengarten, Harry Rasky, Leonard Cohen

to this part of the city. What was the attraction for you? The same kind of thing that seems to appeal to Leonard?"

Mort said, "I guess so, but I first moved to the country. And I had the studio out in the country for the first eighteen years. That was perhaps a bigger switch from Westmount than moving to another part of the city. It can really be rough in the city for a while."

Leonard joined in with the geography. "Funny how we have moved progressively east. First place we took was on Stanley Street. We had an art gallery there. A little gallery called the Four Penny Gallery and it burnt down unfortunately. So we didn't have a place for awhile and then we went to Mountain Street which is a few streets east of that and Mort had a studio for a while on MacKay Street, then that area became much more prosperous and commercial, boutiques and galleries. People stopped living there."

I tried to find out more about Leonard's relationships. His friendships with men are deep and lasting.

"It seems to me having a friend for thirty five years like that, that you would be closer to a man than you can to a woman, someone might say."

"That is possible."

"Why do you think that is?"

"I don't know."

" I think Leonard writes so much about relationships and friendships and all that kind of thing. It's a very tough question but do you know what is it that makes a friend, the quality?"

"I was just thinking about it when you said that thing of thirty five years or whatever, that there are very old friends, both men and women, and the old thing prevails, like the relationship prevails, even if you do not see them or four years at a time. I just got a card from Yakka the other day, who I have not seen for ages. One of the old friends, I spoke to her on the phone a couple of weeks ago."

"Who is Yakka?"

"Yakka is a friend we went to school with. I guess around the early fifties and we were at McGill together. We met at McGill and that friendship has continued over the past, twenty five years."

"I wonder if it is harder to make friends today. Young people seem so alienated or something like that, a different generation."

"Well I think so, friends are friends."

"A group of students who are together for three four years. It was quite an intense period for them, I think that has something to do with it. But years go by and we never hear from each other. But that doesn't seem to impair anything, something has been stamped and sealed a long time ago."

I wanted to know more about where we were at this moment. I asked. Is this a kind of almost ritual coming to this place for breakfast?"

Leonard was pleased to compliment his hosts. "Yeah, it is sort of a nice place to start the day. You know Mr. and Mrs. Solomon have a really great restaurant, just the economy with which they work — it is really instructive — their vehicle is very small you know. You can see they just have a little stove that you could find in anybody's kitchen and a couple of toasters and a couple of pots and they come up with really good meals every day. There is no need for any fancy equipment. They are just what they are."

"It seems to be once again a kind of sparseness that you really seem to like."

"Well it really works, this restaurant. I mean you can feel the hand of the people, Mr. and Mrs. Solomon, you can feel their hand in everything they have here. You know. And they happen to be extraordinary hosts or innkeepers in the real tradition of hospitality. Which, as we know, has nothing to do with furnishing. You know you come in here at six in the morning, and Mr. Solomon will just nod to you. They don't really feel like talking about too much at that time. And they sit down, and your coffee comes and Mr. Solomon will put a *Gazette* in front of you and maybe a cigarillo and Mrs..."

Mort interrupted. "Mrs. Solomon came to see an exhibition I had of drawings and we discovered that she requires the same kind of glasses that I do. She used my glasses to see the work and now if I come in here and I forgot my own glasses, she will hand me the paper and her glasses."

"You know I am going to quote a line from your own book which I like a lot about how the streets change swiftly. 'The skies... with the silhouettes against the St. Lawrence somehow unreal and no one believes it because in Montreal there is no present tense. There is only the past claiming victory.' Like the Solomons seem connected with the past, in that kind of way it seems to me."

Leonard nodded, "Yeah. Well, Mr. Solomon, of course he carries his past with him, it is not too heavy a burden with Mr. Solomon, I do not feel... "

"But you seem to honor that in a way."

His response was deeply Cohen. "Yeah, I like to see the marks on people, I never like the idea of people changing their names. For the same reason you know it is just nice to know where you come from. Well, I think the whole history of Quebec especially is based on the past and that what we see right now in Quebec politics is just the past playing..."

"This seems very much a community."

"Do you know that the motto of Quebec is 'Je me souviens.' I remember."

"Exactly, but is that, well, like a Cohen motto, too?"

"I think it is in a writer, it is in a writer's memory. It could be a writer's motto."

"This seems very much like a community, a village almost, this area in which you live, here in Montreal when you were here."

"Well, I have a lot of friends on the same street. We grew up on the same street too. This particular part of town always has been like a community."

"Yeah."

"Yeah, I think what attracted us to the place is that there is human life going on very visibly and a certain integrity to the community."

"How do you feel when you are in Westmount? Now, like if you visit friends in Westmount, do you feel part of that?"

"Oh, I like to visit friends you know wherever they live, but Westmount is very beautiful. There are lots of parks and trees and streets and everybody seems to be doing fine."

Later, I asked Leonard to read from his novel, *Beautiful Losers*:

Spring comes into Quebec from the west. It is the warm Japan current that brings the change of season to the west coast of Canada. And then the west wind picks it up. It comes across the prairies in the breath of the chinook, waking up the graying and kinds of bearers. It flows over Ontario like a dream of legislation, and it sneaks into Quebec into our villages between our birch trees. In Montreal, the cafes, like a bed of tulip bulbs sprout from their sellers in a display of awnings and sharers.

And then, also in his garden, I suggested he read some favourite poems of mine, the lush words of a sensuous soul.

*You're not supposed to be here
Not supposed to be looking for me
This is the poor side of silence
This is the white noise
        of the abandoned appliance
This is The Captivity*

*You need details
You need the name of a street
You're not supposed to be here
        in the Name of God*

You're waiting for me again
Waiting at the mouth
    of the Tunnel of Love
But where is the cold little river
Where is the painted boat

If only the hummingbird
would sip at your desire
If only the green leaves
could use your longing.
If only a woman were looking
over your shoulder
at a map of the Eternal City

It seems that nothing can take you away
from this odd memorial
Nothing that's been made or born
separate you from
    the fiction of my absence

All the Messiahs are with me in this
You're not supposed to be here
All the Messiahs agree
You're not supposed to be looking for me

He followed without interruption – *The Politics of This Book* — a meditation of mood, a poet's portrait of a state of mind, an incantation of a kindred kind.

Years ago I sat in this garden, at this very table, among the ancestors of yellow daisies that surround me now. I was drugged and happy then. I wrote deep from my sunstroke. Enough of the past. It is a morning in March 1975.
    The bumblebees have arrived. There are noisy birds in the rain gutter.

One thread of a spider web, suddenly white, goes fishing in the sunshine. Some butterflies want to fertilize my shiny boot. A cat sharpens the top of a wall by walking across it, and then by walking back adjusts the horizontal.

I won't be sitting here long. I'm in a terrible hurry. I'm going to Jerusalem. I'm going with the happy Israeli soldiers and I'm going with the King of Saudi Arabia to kneel down in the place that we were promised.

A bee enters a hanging yellow flower like a woman pulling a gown over her head, shivering, struggling upwards. The sun climbs to the middle of the sky and stops. It's noon. The bells of noon ringing loud from the cathedral tower. Great shovelfuls of sound dumped into the grave of our activity. The sound fills up every space and every thought. The past is plugged up. Layer after layer of the present seizes us, buries us in one vast amber paperweight.

I won't be going to Jerusalem after all. You will have to go to Jerusalem alone. It is yours. It was given to you by the angels of culture and time. But I can't go. And I can't loosen your interest in the war. You will want to see corpses, the oldest tourist attraction, and you will want to "challenge the sphincters of your cowardice under sand and fire." Goodbye.

I will be here if you look back, at this very table, in this very garden where the bumblebee charges like a bull into the yellow trumpet, and the sun makes a dent in my black trousers, and my wife repeats on a loop, "Did you smell the ambrosia of the universe in my little cunt?" and the birds tune up at last.

Leonard was in a sense a poet evolving. He was struggling with his role. Dylan, in a way had it easy. America was on fire with unrest, inner city madness. He set it to music. He growled at the dissonance of the divisions. And his audiences were vast and approving.

Leonard, a Canadian, was stuck with commenting on a footnote to world change — the eternal bickering between the French and the English, a problem that causes the eyes of the outsider to gloss over with boredom. Even Byron didn't do too well with political poems. Leonard felt compelled as an observer of his time to suggest a few words in judgement, now almost lost. His attitude was a

plague on both your houses.
First, about the French:

I think you are fools to speak French
It is a language which invites the mind
to rebel against itself causing inflamed ideas
grotesque postures and a theoretical approach
to common body functions. It ordains the soul
in a tacky priesthood devoted to the salvation
of a failed erection. It is the language
of cancer as it annexes the spirit and
installs a tumor in every honeycomb
Between the rotten teeth of French are incubated
the pettiest notions of destiny and the shabbiest
versions of glory and the dreariest dogma of change
ever to pollute the simplicity of human action
French is a carnival mirror in which the
brachycephalic idiot is affirmed and encouraged
to compose a manifesto on the destruction of the sideshow

I think you are fools to speak English
I know what you are thinking when you speak English
You are thinking piggy English thoughts
you sterilized swine of a language that has no genitals
You are peepee and kaka and nothing else
and therefore the lovers die in all your songs
You can't fool me you cradle of urine
where Jesus Christ was finally put to sleep
and even the bowels of Satan cannot find
a decent place to stink in your flat rhythms
of ambition and disease
English, I know you, you are frightened by saliva
your adventure is the glass bricks of sociology

you are German with a license to kill

I hate you but it is not in English
I love you but it is not in French
I speak to the devil but it is not about your Punishment
I speak to the table but it is not about your plan
I kneel between the legs of the moon
in a vehicle of perfect stuttering
and you dare to interview me on the matter
of your loathsome destinies
you poor boobies of the north
who have set out for heaven with your mouths on fire
Surrender now surrender to each other
your loveliest useless aspects
and live with me in this and other voices
like the wind harps you were meant to be
Come and sleep in the mother tongue
and be awakened by a virgin
(O dead-hearted turds of particular speech)
be awakened by a virgin
into a sovereign state of common grace

I was stunned by the harshness of it all, from such a delicate man. It confused me, so I asked, "Why do you feel it necessary to have such violent words to describe words. That's a tough question, but maybe you have an answer." It was something he would not speak about. The speaker had spoken. That was that.

"I don't have an answer. I..."

He became silent. I tried again.

"But people are hearing, that imagery that you have there, might say, well, you have a savage attitude toward language, and you use language to communicate. In the particular tongue, too?'

Leonard withdrew.

"I just can't, I can't beyond, the poem itself. Everything that I have thought about the matter is there and I think the language is appropriate. I wouldn't want to, I wouldn't want to make a commentary."

He kindly changed the subject with another reading that warm summer day, *One of These Days*. Memory vivid, painful memory.

One of these days we're going to get outside. We'll take off your shoes and listen to the wind chimes in the garden. The dust of vanished jet planes will be a glaze around the street lamps. The little star of Karl Marx will light a corner of the vault. We'll lie beside the shed mingling our conversation with the soft round noise of the neighbor's doves. Adam's father will be feeling better. So will Adam's mother. Our rugged life in the back yard is about to begin. We're going to dig a lily pond if we can get outside. You can see us in our chairs now, immensely attractive and paralyzed. There we are reflected in the windows of the room. We'd weep over the story you could tell about us. You'd be so pleased to meet people who do not wish to govern you.

I suggested that, of course, it was written about this very garden. He seemed enormously sad, suddenly so sad.

"Yeah. Yeah, uh, uh, there, the neighbors keep doves up there. Are they still there now? I haven't heard them. They had a chicken?"

It was an afternoon of remembrance. I asked if he had another poem. I felt the hurt of his response.

"Uh, sure."

Slowly I married her
Slowly and bitterly married her love
Married her body
 in her boredom and joy
Slowly I came to her
Slow and resentfully came to her bed
Came to her table

in hunger and habit
  came to be fed
Slowly I married her
sanctioned by none
with nobody's blessings
in nobody's name
  amid general warnings
  amid general scorn
Came to her fragrance
  my nostrils wide
Came to her greed
  with seed for a child
Years in the coming
and years in retreat
  Slowly I married her
Slowly I kneeled
And now we are wounded
  so deep and so well
that no one can hurt us
except Death itself
  And all through Death's dream
I move with her lips
The dream is a night
  but eternal the kiss
And slowly I come to her
  slowly we shed
the clothes of our doubting
  and slowly we wed

I felt like an intruder. It still disturbs me after all this time, his eloquence and emotion. I said: "It seems so tragic. Do you feel the tragedy of it, or, when you read it, or, is tragedy recollected on a sunny day not so terrible?" His response was to continue reading.

A kind of acupuncture of the soul.

This is the language of love, but the language spoken in lower worlds, among the citizens of the broken vessels. Nevertheless, wheels appear and turn, and creatures are moved from here to there. It is a garbled language, the letters weak and badly formed, the parchments stained with excrement; however, we are certain, there is no doubt that it derives from the great formula of letters, formed by a voice, impressed upon the air, and set in the mouth in five places, namely:

male and female, created He them

Last night, while my daughter was sleeping in the room with the blue carpet from the Main, and my son was sleeping in my own bed, Lilith appeared to me. She has never given me up. As usual, I could not resist her. It was close enough to the full moon for me to receive a blemish. I received it in two places.

This morning after taking the children to school, I drove down to the Avis garage, to have snow-tires put on the Datsun. They were amazed that I had been driving all winter without them (it is now the end of January). My power extends no further, but I am grateful for the huge and terrible safety with which He has so far surrounded me. And so it goes, the letters weaker and weaker, the distortions more grotesque, further and further from the voice, deeper and deeper in the Exile.

And now it comes to pass that into this Exile, already swollen with men in their states of disease, their soiled and useless laws, their menstrual songs, their monstrous ideals — a place is cleared beside the filths of masculinity, and women are welcomed into the Exile.

There was desolation about it all. I felt like a trespasser. 'Back away,' I said to myself. But to Leonard I said simply, pointing to a carved stone. "The thing behind you, is that one of your poems?"

Leonard welcomed the change. "That's one of my poems that Rosengarten encased in, uh, granite? The limestone."

"What does it say?"

"It says, 'Each man has a way to betray the revolution. This is mine.'"

"What is that from?"

"I don't know, oh, I think it's from *Energy of Slaves*."

"Okay, cut."

And so we moved on to more pleasant themes and variations.

We went to Westmount, back to the place of his birth. His father's house, his mother's home kept like a shrine. Why?

"Well, the question is, do you still know the people on the street?"

There was an intense quiet about him. "There are some people, who have been here a long time. Across the street, Mr. and Mrs. Leach, they've been here a long time. They kind of watch over the house now."

"It seems very isolated here, uh, to, to a stranger. It seems somehow, removed from the city, is it? It's safe. It's a nice place to bring up kids. Park next door. Not too much traffic on the streets."

"What happened to the other kids, who were brought up with you on the block, do you know?"

"Well, some of them turned out like Mort. Mort, grew up, up the street here, on upper Belmont. Westmount Boulevard separates, upper Westmount from lower Westmount. This is lower Westmount. This is modest Westmount. Above the Boulevard, the great houses start."

Westmount is, of course, an island of privilege on the island of Montreal. It was a haven for the Jews who found luxury before the silent revolution sent them fleeing from nationalism. I began by prying into the level of his own revolution.

"The question, did most of those people just go into the business of their parents, or did they find great daring and seek out the world, or do you have any idea?"

Leonard again, was generous. He would not criticize.

"I never thought of any of the people that I knew here, living conventional lives, any sense that they didn't encounter, or didn't go out to meet any challenges. The people I know that come from here, like my cousins, they seem to be leading approximately the same kind of lives as I do, or Mort does. I really think it makes no difference really to a man whether he goes into art, or whether he goes into business. I don't think those are the real choices that determine the quality of life. I think the challenges are there, and, I don't think there's any way out of the real things that confront people."

The geography of Montreal speaks about its roots and its separateness.

"Where was school from here?"

"It's just a couple of blocks over on Westmount Avenue."

"And there's a Hebrew school, too, right?"

"Hebrew school is just down across the park."

"And the park was the center of activity?"

"We used to play in the park a lot, and we used to cross it, even after I left elementary school, on the way down to high school, Westmount High School, we used to walk through this park."

The park, a Dick and Jane place of memory, a souvenir of a different time, a safe haven where Leonard would play with his sister, his favorite game, the making of fantasy angels in the snow.

Even now, yes even now, as we sat on the front stoop of the home that had been his refuge for all those growing-up years in Montreal, it was easy to hear the story of the past that he seemed to be hearing.

"My sister's name is Esther, but I never really got to know her until we were much older and then I discovered that she is a great spirit, great laughter, great talker and solid in herself and solid behind me and my work, full-grown beauty of the blood just like mother."

The very mention of his mother cast a glow on Leonard. For a time, he was with her, had never left her he said: "My mother died two years ago and I think many people experience this but her presence, of course, has become very strong and I think of her as a very big person — a kind of Chekhovian heroine. She laughed deeply, wept deeply, I remember her whipping around the house singing Russian songs, Jewish songs... A great figure, my friends loved her very much ... she was always there. We would come home at two or three o'clock in the morning and while other adolescents would have to sneak into their houses we would walk boldly into the kitchen and start picking food — french fried potatoes, my mother would come down and sit around with us ... a very warm, large, generous person. The sound of Russian balalaikas seemed to greet us as we entered the happy haunted house."

Nothing had been touched since the death of his mother. Time was stopped. A dozen copies of the *Canadian Jewish News* sat piled on a polished bench inside the front door. The sweet smell of Murphy's oil and lemon furniture polish gave the place a taste of honey and heart. Who can ever leave a happy home?

It was agreed there would be no filming in the house. And, indeed, it would have seemed a kind of sacrilege. There might have been a sign that read "Memory of my past — do not disturb."

Instead we rustled through carefully kept, proudly possessed by his mother, albums of photos of the past in the making from tricycle to bar-mitzvah, the incubating icon, and finally the emerging super-star.

I suppose that in a way, we had intruded. The space had been once occupied by joy. Now a mechanical media had intervened, a kind of cleansing of the mind seemed necessary.

That may very well be why next morning, when we were to have a guided tour of the sometimes-picturesque streets, a rather reluctant subject showed up. Leonard was wearing a short-sleeved yellow YMCA T-shirt. He sat in the extreme corner of a pick-up truck as we drove down the boulevards. He offered mostly monosyllabic answers to questions. I had encountered this kind of reaction before, most memorable in the course of making my classic film on Tennessee Williams. When I told him the church rectory where he had been brought up in Canton Mississippi was gone, he had nightmares and could not talk.

Leonard offered useless details such as the data of the tourist highlights such as "You know when Jacques Cartier came here in the sixteenth century they said their first mass by the light of fireflies."

No fireflies and no mass would be said this Montreal morning. But we did learn the way to Ben's, Leonard's favorite delicatessen.

Fortunately in the finished film, the film editor, Paul Nikolich, had the good sense to use visual material and a song.

It has always been my practice to collect what may seem like random visual images until they are linked in a kind of visual poem.

I can recall when we were filming outside the great stone cathedral for such a sequence, suddenly the sky damaged with effect — the sun and cloud in a minuet. I asked the cameraman, Ken Gregg to divert his camera to the sky. By the time he made the move the effect was gone. He waited. Filming is a waiting game. Meantime, a little old lady emerged from the somber darkness of her prayers and joined the expectant crew — a group of grown men staring at a naked sky. Finally, searching for the magic moment through a piece of smoked glass, the lighting engineer, the jovial Erik Kristensen, called out, "It's coming. It's coming." And suddenly there they were, the sun and clouds singing to each other, in a perfect visual harmony. I commanded "Action." And the duet of delight was filmed. We congratulated each other as the woman asked, wanting to join in the rejoicing, "Is there something special happening in heaven today?" I assured her there was and that seemed to satisfy her and us.

These were shots from a tranquil film montage — morning reflections of the mind, the visuals of thought, now composed and married to Leonard's music:

I tried to leave you. I don't deny. I closed the book on us at least a hundred times. I'd wake up every morning by your side.

The years go by. You lose your pride. The baby's crying so you do not go outside. And all your work is right before your eyes.

Goodnight, my darling. I hope you're satisfied. The bed is kind of narrow, but my arms are open wide. And here's a man still working for your smile.

Through the song we now see a memory of Montreal and a present-day one, street scenes, houses, balconies, graffiti, cafes, children — life.

We then adjourned to the luxury of the Four Seasons Hotel for a swim and an afternoon of poetry readings Leonard began.

"This is Montreal as sighted from the expensive windows of the Four Seasons hotel on Sherbrooke Street. That is the mountain, Mount Royal, that is the cross that is lit up every night. That is the television antennae, the agency through which the merchants have their channels into the bedrooms of the poor. That tower is the medical school in which hideous experiments were performed. The streets, McTavish, Redpath, all the great Scots that came to this city, some of whom are buried in the mountain. These are the streets, the University, Gates, old Victorian mansions."

Beware of what comes out of Montreal. Especially during the winter. It is a force corrosive to all human institutions. It will bring everything down, it will defeat itself. It will establish the wilderness in which the Brightness will manifest again.

We who belong to this city, have never left The Church. The Jews are in The Church as they are in the snow. The most violent atheist radical defectors from the Parti Québécois are in The Church. Every style in Montreal, is the style of The Church. The winter is in The Church. The Sun Life Building is in

The Church. Long ago the Catholic Church became a pebble beside the rock on which The Church was founded. The Church has used the winter to break us and now that we are broken, we are going to pull down your pride. The pride of Canada and the pride of Quebec, the pride of the left and the pride of the right, the pride of muscle and the pride of heart, the insane pride of your particular vision will swell and explode because you have all dared to think of killing people. The church despises your tiny works of death and the church declares that EVERY MAN, WOMAN AND CHILD IS PROTECTED.

Everyone knows that The Church is in Montreal. St. Francis is one of many who came through the snow to repair it, or rather, to repair the appearance of its ruin. Now The Church begins the militant phase: every idea of salvation withers in the Brightness of this blaze."

While changing rolls of film I asked Leonard why he did not seem to like the title, "Poet."

"It's due to the process of cultural advertising which has the same effect as commercial advertising. Certain words become devalued and not only that but many people rush to embrace the description and I just don't like the company."

The exception is always Layton, his beloved poet-pal. And so he read to us:

"This is a poem I wrote for Irving Layton, a long time ago."

Layton, when we dance our freilach
under the ghostly handkerchief,
the miracle rabbis of Prague and Vilna
resume their sawdust thrones,
and angels and men, asleep so long
in the cold places of disbelief,
gather in sausage-hung kitchens
to quarrel deliciously and debate
the sounds of the Ineffable Name.

Layton, my friend Lazarovitch,
no Jew was ever lost
while we two dance joyously
in this French province,
cold and oceans west of the temple,
the snow canyoned on the twigs
like forbidden Sabbath manna;
I say no Jew was ever lost
while we weave and billow the handkerchief
into a burning cloud,
measuring all of heaven
with our stitching thumbs.

Reb Israel Lazarovitch,
you no-good Romanian, you're right!
Who cares whether or not
the Messiah is a Litvak?
As for the cynical,
such as we were yesterday,
let them step with us or rot
in their logical shrouds.
We've raised a bright white flag,
and here's our battered fathers' cup of wine,
and now is music
until morning and the morning prayers
lay us down again,
we who dance so beautifully
though we know that freilachs end.

"Some of your critics say that your early stuff is excess. How do you feel about that kind of comment?"

"I love those kind of comments. I love to hear what the critics say, and I always feel that the critics are on trial. I always look carefully at the criticism that comes my way. I don't search it out, but whenever I read a criticism, I read it as a piece of writing, and I judge it by the highest standards of writing, and I generally find it wanting. But I love to hear people speak badly of me."

I didn't know once again if he was toying with me.

"Really? Not really?"

"Critics, critics, I don't have a special vendetta against critics, but, I like to see the way they write. And it's very interesting that, often people who write so badly, presume to measure the standards of others. Now and then, a critic comes along, and they are as rare as good poets, good critics. I'd like to be a critic."

"There's a guy here who writes about sexuals," says Cohen. "Not bisexuals, but sexuals. Do you think that's true? I mean, that's a line from a writer."

"I, I don't know what one of them is."

"A sexual," Cohen says, "does not deal with homosexual, heterosexual, bisexual, simply the sexual."

"Oh, I see, what he means is just treating the sexual force, or the sexual energy."

And the film ran out and I wrote we went to the "wild track" and had a splendid swim in the outdoor pool of the Four Seasons. This was our season. Back in his spare apartment, his comfort zone, I felt we could settle in. His apartment was astonishingly simple as was his Hydra hideaway. I asked about his color, or lack of color scheme.

"Well I don't know... I suppose I could establish some metaphysical reason for it all, but I always preferred rooms like this. Whenever I had the choice, I generally painted the walls white and the floors gray and had, you know, a good table, a couple of good tables, and a chair or two and it allows you to keep track of things. It's nice to have an exterior that is somewhat ordered when the inside is somewhat disordered."

It seemed to have clear, white logic.

"Okay, do you write a lot of your music here, or a lot of your poems here?"

He had an extreme comfort level here.

"I have done a lot of work here. This table has been very good. I had that across the street too. And the kitchen table is a good table."

"You move around a great deal, from place to place. Is there some inner reason for that or is it just a matter because where the work is?"

"That is part of it. I have been moving around a lot in the past ten years, but I am kind of tired of it now. I'd like to stay in one place for a while now."

And, indeed, he would settle in as time passed, but more in Los Angeles, closer to the music scene.

"I was mentioning to you, I saw this Janice Joplin film and somebody asked her why she moved and she says, well she has been looking for her life. But I do not know whether that is just a trite thing to say, in terms of people who travel a lot. But do you feel any sense of that?"

"No, I don't feel the sense of the quest or the odyssey. There just seems to be a reason to move, none of them very profound. You follow the work and, of course, as a musician, there is a lot of moving that goes along with touring and the things that are appropriate to the profession. But I think I would move around a bit, anyhow. But now I don't want to move around."

"In trying to understand what is a poet, the question I always kind of ask is — are you looking for peace of mind or avoiding it?"

"I never question myself with those kind of questions. It seems to me that, you know, daily life has enough perplexities, just handling the ordinary events. I don't really examine it from that point of view. I don't feel myself on a mission or I am certainly not. I think everybody has the notion of their own destiny, I mean a vague notion, an indescribable notion. But I see it from the daily point of view, of keeping things neat as possible."

"I just wonder about your answer to that...you have no sense of mission, you do or do not...would you say?"

"Well, I find a sense of mission difficult to speak about. It is like one's religion. Or one's own rapport with the Holy Order, and it's almost impossible to speak of. In fact, it's dangerous and foolhardy to speak of it. You see, then it loses its power, its sanctity. It is really as one feels about one's own divine role. I mean every man feels a certain sense of how he relates to the whole mess. And I think the song is the appropriate place to examine those kinds of questions or the work. I never felt that conversation really is the appropriate arena for the examination of those kinds of inquiries."

"Well, is what you are saying that the poem, the song is the release for that expression of things that other people just try and express in words, in their daily conversation?"

Out of his answer would come the title of the film, the song, the work, the life, perhaps the meaning.

"It's another one of those questions, what the song is. You know it's many things. For one thing it's one's metier, one's work. You do it, you know the best you can. What the profound genesis of that activity is, I really don't know."

I was really curious about how Leonard the poet became Leonard the pop star.

"When we met many years ago, you were not a singer. How did the singing come about? That has always struck me. There must be a story there."

"These problems of the genesis of activity I find difficult. I was always a singer, always played guitar, since I was fourteen or fifteen. I never thought of myself as a singer, in any sense. I had finished *Beautiful Losers* in Greece. I was broke. I had been listening to a lot of country and western music on the Armed Forces radio station in Greece and I started writing a few tunes. I had collected folk songs and been singing for a long time, so I started writing a few down and I was completely unaware of what was happening in North America at the time, which was the great renaissance of music with people like Judy Collins and Dylan and Phil Oakes. I was completely unaware of these people and I came back to Montreal, still pretty much unaware. I started writing a few tunes and I came down to New York and I announced to my friends one evening that I was going to become a pop singer. I was on my way down to Nashville and I wanted to become a country and western singer. In New York I met Judy Collins and a few other people and I saw what was happening and some people got interested in the stuff. Judy got interested in some of the material and recorded it and you know before I knew it, I was in the studio, making my own record."

(Perhaps, you could say the rest is history. Not quite yet. Much later, Judy Collins was to write to him on his birthday! "Know that you have been an ageless inspiration to me. I sing your beautiful, moving, timeless and transformational songs. That is your gift to me.")

But now this humid summer, Montreal days. I wanted very much to go deeper into his connection with this place we were in.

"You know in the *Favorite Game*, which is one of my favorite books of yours, you say, some say that no one ever leaves Montreal for that city like Canada itself, is designed to preserve the past, a past that happened somewhere else. I think that is a terrific description of many things, do you still feel that? It was written a long time ago. Looking back?"

"Well I am just trying to remember now what I meant by that. What did I mean by that?"

"Well at the time I presume that you meant that you could not find any past that you could grab hold of here in a way, or it was too fleeting, or you had to find it somewhere else. I just wonder if it is that what started your wanderings."

"I think I meant by that, that in Montreal, everybody here, if you ask them what they are they will give you a race or a nation, that is not Canadian. They will say they are Hungarian, or Greek or Jewish or and I think Montreal had the real federal idea. I don't know if it has any more, but it had the real federal idea in the most transcendent aspect of that idea and that is that nothing had to be given up by the people that came here. And that the city itself was designed to protect the past, that the European past, or that wherever the people came from, it still operates quite effectively. I think it is about to change, maybe the character of the city will even overwhelm any program to homogenize it. But certainly in the old days, when Montreal was a place where people lived as they lived in other places. And, safely."

But why would he have given up the green luxury of Westmount? As someone who tried to escape the concrete dirt of inner city life, I asked: "I wonder why is it that you have come here, to this particular place? Because it seems to have something, some history? This area seems to have some history and the boards are old and the houses are old and there is some sense that something happened here before."

"Yeah, I guess that is part of it. I think it is a really nice place to live. You know there is that little square that used to be called Carré Vallière, now it is called Parc du Portugal. It is just a really nice place to live. You are close to the street, you have got a little park to sit in. Cookies is across the street for coffee and Mr. and Mrs. Soloman. And, the Main is right there. It is alive."

So now again, his family. Who were they?

"Can we talk a little bit about your own past. Like where did your parents come from? Were they born here?"

"My father was born here and my mother was from Lithuania."

"Was there anything in their history that would indicate a kind of flow of creative spirits or would you have to go back into you ancestry? Do you know anything about that, whether there were poets, singers, whatever in the past?"

"My mother's father was a writer. His name was Rabbi Solomon

Klinetsky and he was a grammarian. He was called the 'Prince of Grammarians.' He stayed at my house, my childhood house, during the last year of this life. He was writing a dictionary without any reference books, just starting it and moving down — he wrote *A Lexicon of Hebrew Homonyms* and *Treasures of Talmudic Interpretations* which were standard textbooks until I guess the Israelis started determining the course of the language. My mother was a good singer, a much better singer than I am and she used to sing around the house quite a bit. She usually moved from melancholy to singing. My father's father was a businessman who believed in the aristocracy of the intellect — that was one of his phrases that he used to use a lot. So there has been a lot of affirmation for that kind of work in my family."

"You say your mother moved from melancholy to singing. Is that what you said?"

"Yes, you know, she was good Chekhovian spirit. Often a lot of the conversation had to do with the disaster of other people's misfortune, regret, like one of the *Three Sisters*. But from time to time, she would sing and she sang beautifully. She had a contralto voice."

"So the singing was a kind of release for her own melancholy. Why did she have that melancholy you think, looking back at it now, it is a long time ago?"

"Well I think that the normal abrasive quality of daily life was enough to plunge her into melancholy from time to time. Especially if one's nature is determined that way."

"Do you think of yourself as being melancholy?"

"I often indulge myself in a melancholy high. That would be a good title for a song, Melancholy High."

"Well that is why I sort of..."

Leonard was getting impatient with my line of questioning – the digging into the archeology of his soul. He picked up his guitar and began searching for a song.

"Is that how songs come like that?"

"Songs."

"Just, you know, a phrase hits you?"

"I generally find the song arises out of the guitar playing, just fooling around on the guitar. Just trying different sequences of chords, really just like playing guitar every day and singing until I make myself cry, then I stop. You know sometimes it happens right away."

"You really sing until you make yourself cry, Leonard?"

"Sometimes. I don't weep copiously, but you know, I just feel a little catch in my throat or something like that. Then I know that I am in contact with something that is that just a little deeper than where I started when I picked the guitar up."

I began again. His roots.

"How important do you think your being Jewish is in what you do?"

"Well, to have had the privilege of knowing an old tradition. It has been, I think, decisive in my own life."

"But in some of your poems, especially your early poems, it seems almost obsessive, I would think it does seem that way. Can you explain that a little more?"

"Well, the Bible is, I guess, the most important book in my life. So, I don't know if I had been a Christian or whether it would have the same significance. I know Christians for whom the Bible has that significance. It was the English Bible, that language, that touched me, those concerns the way the voice is raised for instance in the songs, or lamentations, the sense of grandeur in the prophets, the sense of chaotic revelation in the *Book of Revelations*. Those kinds of modes of speech, where the heart is beating fast, there is no other book that has that scope. It really touched me, the Jewish Liturgy, the sound of the Jewish voice raised in prayer, or adoration or praise, those are the kinds of modes that touched me and that informed me."

Again, he wanted a change. He picked up the guitar again. A

punctuation, a segue into another aspect of the forces that molded him. I asked.

"What are you doing, is that you fiddling or what?"

"Just fiddling."

"But you know when I listen to you playing the guitar and we are talking about the kind of things inspired by it...too often, the music, it seems to me, that am I not hearing right. Like it sounds very Spanish, what you are doing now."

There followed a kind of Leonard Cohen explanation. Accept it or not. "Yeah, yeah. The only guitar lessons I had were from a man I met when I was fifteen. He was a flamenco player and I met him in the park and I heard him playing. He was playing in the park and I asked him to give me a few lessons and he taught me. I think he just taught me this sequence which went ...something like that. And then he committed suicide shortly afterwards and those, just those two chords and the touch he had, I don't know. I think they gave me most of the stuff I know. He taught it to me— just one or two lessons, I don't want to describe myself as a guitarist because I am not really a very good guitarist, but just the feel he had for the instrument, and the chord sequences. I think I have based a lot of my songs on just those little movements."

"Could you give me an example of that in one of your songs."

Searching. Searching for explanations of what may not be explainable. Leonard responded:

"Ah, like *Gypsy Wife*...that kind of thing you know. That is a new song."

"Would that song have started as a poem, and then a song, or was it the music and then the words coming together?"

Try again. Let us find origins. He strummed the guitar, finding an instant gratification perhaps.

"I love those moments when writers describe how their songs started. They usually were totally inaccurate, but they are always interesting to hear. That particular song started in a woman's apartment last winter. My marriage was breaking up and she had a guitar. I was waiting for her to get ready and that is exactly what I was thinking, 'where, where is my gypsy wife tonight?' And, it was one of those songs that started that way, most of them, are much less fluent in their beginnings, but it was just... thinking to myself...that one happened very easily and I got that sequence. I guess you could find it a lot in Spanish or eastern music."

"On that same new album there is a song that I particularly like which seems very spiritual and religious, *Through the Window* is it...could you just do a little of it? Is it easy?"

Demons and angels?

"Oh yeah...I can't quite get up to that note this summer. I don't think I can get up there."

"But, a lot of people might say that you sing in praise of lonesomeness, do you?"

"In praise of lonesomeness?"

"Yeah. That is the common phraseology, Leonard Cohen sings in praise of lonesomeness."

"Well, you get some good reviews and you get some bad reviews."

"No, but I just wonder about your attitude towards that attitude about you. I don't not find that, myself, but I wonder what your own feeling is about that view of some of your stuff. What I am trying to get at, Leonard, is do you feel that there is a large area of misunderstanding? Whether it is your book, the poetry and the song? Is it together?"

"I don't think so, I never really felt misunderstood. I think that people... not only with my work, but with any work that touches the heart, and when one is successful, it's very hard to speak about it. It's like speaking about a kiss or an embrace. You know perfectly well what is going on, in the midst of it, when it's over. You are asked to describe it from many points of view."

"But, it really has nothing to do with the experience and I think when a song is true, that it communicates immediately and then when people come out of the song and through the natural habit of investigation, and enjoing themselves to describe what has happened or whether why they liked it or why they didn't like it, they get into explanations of you know whether it's melancholy or it's..."

His thought trailed off. I urged him to continue.

"Well one of the things that prompted the question is I think a line from *Death of a Lady's Man*, where you say, 'it will become clear that I am the stylist of my era and the only honest man in town,' and I was wondering what you were thinking about when you wrote that particular line, if you can recall?"

He seemed shy in his response.

"Well, I think that that paragraph is written extravagantly and is meant to have that kind of inflated arrogant tone to it. Not to be taken altogether seriously except in my most self-indulgent moments. 'I am the stylist of my era and the only honest man in town.' There are moments when I do feel that way. Then you know when I put my work up against Solzenitshyn's and others, I find the statement ludicrous. Maybe I was thinking of the critics, not too often fortunately, but sometimes...you get angry. Now there is a little bit of anger in there. Sometimes I feel that my work in North America has to be justified. In a lot of reviews that I have read, a lot of people I come across, they don't think that I can sing at all, and many of the reviews concentrate on that fact, rather than examining what might be in front of them, which is the work of a stylist. In Europe where they have a tradition and in Quebec also, of the *chansonier*, or the speaker of the song, just the sound of the man's voice and how esthetically it is his own voice that really determines the excellence of the work. So that I have run into some trouble with people feeling unless you hit every note right on, and you have a certain polished sound to the voice, it corresponds to all the other polished sounds, to the polished voices, that you hear all the time, unless it satisfies those criteria, you really aren't singing. So from time to time, I feel compelled to remind people, not too many, I don't have a chip on my shoulder, it's not even an important thing, but I feel compelled to remind people that there is such a thing as a style, that might be escaping their notice."

While the cameraman was reloading the film, I decided to make some observations about the few, very few, objects that lay around — a gold figure of a nude woman, about the size of an ashtray, for instance, a splendid chunk of art deco.

"Just before you begin, that statue on the table, that we are looking at there, I just wonder where it came from. It is so elegant."

Leonard decided he would have a little fun with me.

"Well, it came from Caplan's, which is across the street. It is a hardware store. And, Mr. Caplan had a warehouse and his lawyer advised him to close it up because of the overhead and when they were cleaning it up, they found a box of these plaster cast little statues done by an Italian sculptor called...Petrucci in the twenties or thirties in Montreal and he told me that the Petruccis were two brothers who came over here and decided to make a killing by making little statuettes and they sold a few of them and I think they died of alcoholism in the flush of success. I think they are very beautiful. I have another one which is over there. They were about three dollars each and I bought a whole box of them. I have about twenty of the other ones. This is the only one of this kind, though. There is a black one still in the store, painted black and this is the only bronze one."

"Well you seem to be a collector of inexpensive things, in a kind of way, and I think if it had cost three thousand, maybe you would not have bought it."

Leonard laughed at the idea, a real laugh. "Well I definitely wouldn't have bought it if it had cost three thousand. But they are beautiful. That man really loved women. I am going to give you one, Harry."

"Okay, I would value that."

Indeed to this day I keep this precious unprecious work of art near my bed, as a memento.

"Would you read a poem that happened here?"

"Okay, these are not very good poems, but they are about the people around here."

I don't suppose you care to know
But they planted twelve ash trees in the Parc du Portugal
We took that maverick maple that grew from seed
beside the flower bed
And planted it in Cheryl's yard.
Michelle and Maureen have cleaned and planted
out back and put in a sapling
Mr. and Mrs. DeLuca have taken out their small
trees that they kept in the basement all winter
They stand in old wine barrels
The maple tree in front of the house has put
out small orange claws
Into the harmless spring breezes
The upturned branches of the lonely poplar on the block
Have on their undergarments of green mist
Needless to say we have all come outside like the
laundry
I sit on this rotten balcony looking down at the
little trees
Recently brought forth from the wine dark basement
of Mr. and Mrs. DeLuca.
Quite pleased to be here.
Old friends nearby in their various rooms
And doorsteps and balconies
I would like to make my lifework as finely carved as your nostril
As wild and mysterious as you disappearance from
my life

As implacable as you hatred
As stubborn in beauty as your flight from hearth and family.

"A better view of that would be from that little balcony up there, Mr. and Mrs. Deluca live downstairs. They make wine. Very good wine. There is a lot of booze made on this street.

"Do you have another?" I suppose I was stunned by the personal nature of the poem of response.

"This comes out of sitting on that little balcony, off my kitchen here. I haven't read these for a long time, so I might stumble over them. And I certainly don't defend the position of many of these."

They will be rich for a long time
The hearts of their children will be even harder
than their own hardened hearts
We will be fighting for a long time over the wine
My twelve year old daughter on the balcony
is singing a song concerning these matters
It is She whom our grand-parents meant
when they invoked The Virgin
It has nothing to do with that Place of Hers
which will be filled, naturally, with men's tears
We fight with Her strength, The Virgin's strength
and we hope with The Virgin's hope
Because we have fed on the garbage of the rich
we have thought of a world without corruption
Because we have bowed so much
and pretended so much
we have thought of a different world
We know the world does not change
We know the rich do not give up
We know the rich
Their voices are loud and their strength is mighty

But in every one of our houses there is A Virgin
And we don't care
whom She pleasures
behind the chicken coop
We have The Virgin
and she tells us:
Do not live in the world
So we dig in and we arm ourselves
with the smile of The Virgin
and the scorn of The Virgin
and the muscled hope of The Virgin
and because we do not live in the world
we can see it and we can reach for it
and we can pluck it out of the sky
That is our strategy against the rich
who grow slowly stupid among their possessions.
Who have forgotten
that there is an edge to the world
and that many live and watch them from beyond it
This is what she sings about
Our Seamstress of the Torn
as She draws the neighbor's son
away from the repairing
of his broken bicycle
to be astounded by Her new breasts

"Do you have another, before we lay that to rest? Or we can move on to something else, if you want."

Women and thoughts of women have somehow had a profound effect on the work of Cohen.

"The question of the man who made that statue...you said he really liked women. Do you really like women? Would you say all your poems and songs...mostly they are women's names or dedicated to women, or love of women."

"One is deeply concerned with women. Of course. I got completely obsessed by women. Have been for as long as I can remember."

"Why?"

"I don't know why."

"Well obviously you have reflected on that, I would think."

Leonard became surprisingly defensive.

"I have been too busy to reflect on that. I think everybody is like that, I mean all men are like that, aren't they? They think continually of women. And they think continually of us. I think it's the divine scheme. It is a beautiful thing, for us to be so deeply interested in each other."

"In your audiences, is there a ratio of how many male to female? Are they mostly female?"

"I haven't noticed that, no. I am not so interested in women any more. I don't think. You have to write about something, and women stand for the objective world. For a man they stand for the thing that you are not and that is what you always reach for, in a song."

"Do you know where all these women are that you have written about?"

"Yeah, I know where everybody is. I mean all my friends, I keep close contact with my friends."

"But there are many who passed in the night."

"I don't know about that. I mean that probably is true, you know, but I tend to remember the people that I have come close to."

"Do you get much mail from people you do not know?"

"I get a few letters. The letters don't come pouring in or anything like that, but there is always a few letters a week. Sometimes more, you know. When you put out a record somehow, or a book, it revives the correspondence."

As the afternoon moved on we switched locales, from one white-on-white area to another. There was a sense of loneliness about him, I thought. And I tried to investigate this aspect of his being. How could someone who seemed so desirable to almost all women seem to be so solitary? Perhaps that would emerge as the days on tour went on. Now it was a time to be specific about certain songs, for instance what has become his signature song.

"Could you talk about the individual songs, *Bird on the Wire* — what did you remember about the circumstance of writing it, where did it come from?"

"*Bird on the Wire*. I began that song in Greece. The melody began a few of the lyrics, a few of the lines. And then it was still with me. I was in Los Angeles. I was living in a motel on the Sunset strip — it developed a little further. Then I made a recording of it which David Crosby produced. Ah, I never finished that recording. And the song continued to develop. I made a recording of it in Nashville with Bob Johnson as producer. And apparently the lyrics still weren't finished. I changed the lyrics and a different lyric appears in a record called *Live Songs*. And then the lyric changed again somewhat in the most recent treatments of the song — so it's continued being written for about eight or nine years."

"The line — 'I have tried in my way to be free'— can you amplify that just a bit?"

"I don't think there's much to say about that Harry. It's as explicit as you can get. It mitigates a kind of arrogant human statement, which is 'I have tried to be free' – well everybody has tried to be free. 'In my way' somewhat modifies and softens the idea, and also includes the possibility of failure. Because you say, you know, according to my own light and in my way I've tried, and I've messed it up like everybody else, but that was the effort."

"Moving on to the *Chelsea Hotel*. When was that and how did that come about?'

"I began that song, I would say ah, the very late sixties. I'm not quite sure when I began the song. There is a version of it that I made in 1972, that I never released. It went through a lot of changes I don't think it was ready to record until 1974. My meeting Janis Joplin at the Chelsea Hotel was the genesis or the seed of the song. It went through a lot of changes. That's about it."

"In introducing it, it's one of the, the only one I believe that you always dedicate to Janis Joplin.'"

He spoke quickly and reflectively.

"As the years went by I began to realize that it was Janis Joplin who gave me the seed of the song. Often a song develops from the gift of another individual, as though somebody hands you the song. It may take years to develop. Like the song *Nancy*. I remember its genesis very, very clearly. It was someone I met in an all night diner in Nashville. And I was working on the song and I couldn't break it. And I remember just standing at the jukebox looking at the selection of songs and a young woman came up and stood beside me and said, 'You ought to play R7.' And I spoke to her for a moment and I realized that some kind of transfer was being made, that the heart was being softened in some way by the presence of this other person. And in a sense the seed of the song was being handed over. Well, while I was working on the song I wasn't even sure it was the song Janis Joplin had given me but as I began working on it I understood what that seed, the seed gift, or the seed origin or the genesis, that thing from which the song develops, that softens the heart enough to receive ah, whatever the energies are that produce the song, that it was Janis Joplin. And as the years went by I began to want to acknowledge that gift."

And so, sitting on his narrow bed, a fedora on his head and a glass of brandy nearby, he sang for us a ballad of remembrance.

Perhaps now was the time to test him with a simple, but complex question.

"A difficult question — there's a line in that song, 'I don't mean to suggest that I loved you the best' might suggest that it's very hard for you to love any person the best or, or is that not..."

He switched the direction of the question with his answer. "Well, that specifically meant that I wasn't one of Janis Joplin's closest friends. I don't really know her life deeply. I'd bump into her now and then and I knew her slightly, but there was obviously some kind of rapport and I did feel some sort of closeness to her — but I didn't want to include myself for history's sake or accuracy's sake as one of her intimates. I wasn't."

Photo: © Hazel Field

I persisted: " But generally in terms of the life of Leonard Cohen is, 'I don't mean to suggest that I love you the best,' I wonder how often you feel that about wonderful women you've known."

"Well, I, you know, not to advertise my own famous modesty, I think it's accurate. I don't mean to suggest that I loved you the best, I mean I think there are people who love others, especially in this particular case, loved you better than I could or did. Because time also is a degree in the estimation of love, and there are people she knew well, and who supported her and I would say that to many, of many people that I've known."

And that was that. This day, that question, perhaps too intimate and unfair would not be answered.

"Okay we're going to move on to another song, which — it seems to me — sounds like a particular event. I don't know if I'm correct or not, *Famous Blue Raincoat*?"

"*Famous Blue Raincoat*. I finished the lyric for that song in New York in a loft on Clinton St. I think I mention Clinton St. There's music on Clinton St. all through the evening. I began the melody for that song around 1968. I remember playing it for my mother in her kitchen before it had a lyric. She said she liked the tune. The lyric developed somewhat later. I think it was in the early seventies, maybe. I was living with Marianna in a loft on Stanton St. and I remember the notebook, it was a blue covered notebook. And I began writing. In fact I have the notebook over there I think."

And so it was. There was a sparse collection of items in this sparsely furnished, secluded place.

What is the significance of the photograph or drawing behind you Leonard? It was indeed a simple drawing.

"I think it's an etching. Let's see what is that? My grand uncle gave me that. My grandmother's brother. He gave me that after my grandmother died and he was breaking up the flat where she lived. He gave me a number of things. That, that desk also was my grandmother's desk. But he gave me that picture. I always thought it was beautiful. I guess I'd admired it when I was a child running around my grandmother's house and he gave it to me."

"You have a photograph of him?"

"Yes, he was a world traveler. He was a wonderful man and he was the kind of uncle that all the grandchildren loved most. He took real interest in the grandchildren, and played games with us, and showed us his diary. He kept a meticulous journal on everything he'd done, each day of his life and he'd say, 'Would you like to know what I did in 1925 on January 11?' And he'd be able to tell you what he did. We took a trip to Egypt, and the Holy Land around... it must have been 1911 or so. And he was photographed as tourists were in those days on a camel in front of the Great Sphinx, or the pyramids."

It was the kind of photo every tourist takes in Egypt, camel shot number one. We moved on.

"The book behind you...what is that?"

"This book is a book written by my mother's father — my grandfather. It's a book in Hebrew. It's a Hebrew dictionary called *A Lexicon of Hebrew Homonyms* with interpretations of meaning, grammatical analysis and adequate reverences by Rabbi Solomen Klinetsky, author of *Treasures of Talmudical Interpretations*, which is a thesaurus of Talmudic intepretation."

"That photograph of him...he's very distinguished looking fellow. You remember him vividly?"

"I remember him very well because he spent the last year or so of his life in Montreal. Usually he lived in New York City where he had access to his old cronies. But he died in Montreal and I knew him well the last months of his life."

"Do you think the weight of Talmudic scholarship is part of your own searching for meanings of things?"

"No. I had started to write when I met him. I guess it was the first two or three years. And he indicated some interest. He was not at his best in his last few years but he did indicate some sort of sense of solidarity and pleasure that I was writing because he was actually working on a dictionary, another dictionary. He was living in the room next to mine, and I was tapping away at my typewriter and he was writing this dictionary, without any reference books, incidentally, he was just starting at A and going on. I don't exactly know what the dictionary was about, but he was a distinguished scholar. And it's interesting that A.M. Klein reviewed his book when it came out. So it was, it had some weight in that world at the time. But ah no, his example...except that there was another writer in the family as an encouragement. You know I didn't really know him that well so that he would be a real continuing influence."

We turned to another photo, an affable man with a military moustache.

"The photographs of your father have him in uniform. What was that?"

There was a certain pride in his response — a son claiming the strength of a father who died too young.

"My father and my uncle, many of my cousins volunteered for service in the first World War. I'm not sure, I think my father was one of the first commissioned officers, first Jewish commissioned officers, in the Canadian Army. They were very patriotic men and very much in favor of Empire and saw it as their duty and took great pride in it."

"Which brings me to the next song *Field Commander Cohen*. Did you play with those medals? Did it have anything to do with your interest, and the title of this song? Can you describe the circumstances of Field Commander Cohen?"

His answer has surprised many who think of Leonard as strictly a spiritual being:

"I don't quite remember the genesis of that song, except that Field Commander is an ironic description, although I always loved the army. And my father had intended to send me to the Kingston Military Academy actually. And if he'd have lived, I would probably have been in the Canadian Army. *Field Commander*, in the sense, I think that grew from touring, in the sense that when you're on tour, it is that kind of leadership, rather than any executive leadership, because you are on the field, and it is moment to moment decisions. And you do have a group of men and women to keep together under sometimes strenuous circumstances."

Field Commander Cohen, he was our most important spy, wounded in the line of duty, parachuting acid into diplomatic cocktail parties, urging Fidel Castro to abandon fields and castles, leave it all, and, like a man, come back to nothing special, such as waiting rooms, and ticket lines, and silver bullet suicides, and messianic ocean tides, and racial roller-coaster rides, and other forms of boredom advertised as poetry. I know you need your sleep now, I know your life's been hard, but many men are falling where you promised to stand guard.

I never asked but I heard you cast your lot along with the poor. How come I overheard your prayer that you be this and nothing more than some grateful, faithful woman's favorite singing millionaire, the patron saint of envy and the grocer of despair, working for the Yankee dollar? I know you need your sleep now, I know your life's been hard, but many men are falling where you promised to stand guard.

Lover, come and lie with me, if my lover is who you are. And be your sweetest self a while, until I ask for more, my child. Then let the other selves be sung, yes, let them manifest and come 'til every taste is on the tongue, 'til love is pierced and love is hung, and every kind of freedom done, then oh my love, oh my love, oh my love, oh my love.

"I wonder if it has anything to do with what seems to be almost a love of hardship, for instance you have that stove behind you, which seems quite humble, if you like."

Leonard mocked my stories for meaning. It would not come simply.

"This stove is far from humble. This is one, an advanced design of stove and it supplies extremely adequate and generous heat to my apartment. This is not humble, this is an advanced design."

I was obviously going nowhere with this line of interrogation. The answer would come in other ways.

"I'm going to move on to another song which I think, has a

very complex beginning, *The Guests*."

"*The Guests*. One by one the guests arrive, the guests are coming through. The open-hearted many, the broken-hearted few.'"

"Where did that come from? Wasn't it connected with a Persian poet or something like that?"

"I think that kind of imagery can be discovered all through literature. The Persian poet Rumi uses the idea of the guests a lot. The festival, the feast and the guests. It's almost impossible to talk about that seed moment of when a song begins. You know, this is far from the song. I could describe the song, but it's far from the song. It could be the soul comes into the world... there's some notion that the soul has a feast, is a festival, that there is a banquet. It strives to experience the hospitality of the world. It doesn't achieve it, it feels lonely. This is everybody's experience. It feels lost. It stumbles around on the outskirts of the party. If the striving is deep enough, or if the grace of the host is turned towards the seeking guest, then suddenly the inner door flies open and he finds himself, the soul finds himself at the banquet table, although no one knows where the night is going and no one actually understands the mechanics of this grace except that we experience it from time to time."

It was a song that did and does haunt me, like wild flowers of extraordinary beauty, purple and pink and white, in the tall grass of our lives. "It's become a very popular song I think in France, has it not?"

"It's curious about that song — I think it's because of the chorus, and Jennifer Warnes beautiful arrangement of the vocal chorus that gives the song some potential for popularity."

"All right, so we move on to *The Gypsy Wife* — where, where, where is my gypsy wife tonight?"

"*The Gypsy Wife*."

He played the chord on his guitar, a longing look to an unknown place.

"Where, where, where is my gypsy wife tonight? Well, well, I have to preface all exposition of these songs by saying there really is no footnote to the song because if I felt there was a footnote to the song, I would have included that information in the song itself. I'm interested in the song standing without footnotes or commentaries. And that's the mark of a completed song — that it doesn't need anything else said about it. But just for ancillary or auxiliary information you could say the song is written to my gypsy wife, or the wife that is gone, or to the woman that is gone. You could look at it as the woman is gone from personal life...

See, ah *The Gypsy Wife* was one of the last and swiftest songs I've written. I started it in Los Angeles around the time I began recording, which was last March or April. And the song was ready in about three months. And of course my own marriage was breaking up at the time and in a sense it was written for my gypsy wife, in other words for the wife that was wandering away. But in another way it's just a song about the way men and women have lost one another. That men and women have wandered away from each other and have become gypsies to each other. The last verse says – 'there is no man or woman you can touch, but you who come between them will be judged!' In other words even though we are in the midst of some kind of psyche catastrophe it's not an invitation to take advantage of it and that's mostly what the song is about."

The conversation was flowing fast.

"There is a war between...?"

"...the rich and poor... there is a war between the rich and poor, there is a war between a man and a woman. That's an earlier version and I guess a less charitable version of the predicament. But it's important to have that because even in the midst, in the midst of this flood, or catastrophe which we are in these are the days of the flood, these are the final days. In a sense all the institutions are and have been swept away. And the ethical question is what is the proper behavior, what is the appropriate behavior in the midst of a catastrophe, in the midst of a flood. That song was a kind of war-cry to strengthen the participants to inform them that there was a conflict. But it's an uncharitable song and it's very difficult to sing it correctly, without making it sound like a slogan, without having it informed by bitterness. There is a proper way to sing it. I don't think I've discovered the right way."

"Is there a war between them — men and women? Do you agree?"

"Well, there is a war. There's no question about it that the truth has been dissolved. There's lots of reasons previous to these present moments for upholding the truth between men and women. They're lots of things needed to be done in common, and in community and in communion, but those reasons have dissolved so that the war became clear, it broke out in everybody's mind. I think that's a very primitive and elementary view of the situation."

"*The Window* is a new song, I think."

"Yea, Yea."

Why do you stand by the window
abandoned to beauty and pride?
the thorn of the night in your bosom,
the spear of the age in your side;
lost in the rages of fragrance,
lost in the rags of remorse,
lost in the waves of a sickness
that loosens the high silver nerves.

O chosen love, O frozen love
O tangle of matter and ghost.
O darling of angels, demons and saints
and the whole broken-hearted host –
    Gentle this soul.

Come forth from the cloud of unknowing
and kiss the cheek of the moon;
the code of solitude broken,
why tarry confused and alone?
And leave no word of discomfort,
and leave no observer to mourn,
but climb on your tears and be silent
like the rose on its ladder of thorn.

Then lay your rose on the fire;
the fire give up to the sun;
the sun give over to splendor
in the arms of the High Holy One;
for the Holy One dreams of a letter,
dreams of a letter's death –
oh bless the continuous stutter
of the word being made into flesh.

O chosen love, O frozen love
O tangle of matter and ghost.
O darling of angels, demons and saints
and the whole broken-hearted host –
    Gentle this soul,
    gentle this soul.

"Was that a visual image that developed that song I wonder. Why do you stand by the window abandoned to beauty and pride? Was it something you say?"

"I tried many, many versions of that song and I was trying to write a lyric for that for over a year and I have many, many versions of the song, of the lyric. The melody I established quite early and I liked it. Right behind you on that desk is a pile of pages of attempted lyrics for that melody. You know, it's hard to isolate, indicate or explain that precise moment when that kind of very accurate and explicit language that we call poetry arrives and satisfies you because it's really based on the harmonics of that language, rather than the words themselves."

"There's a lot of images in those particular lyrics — of darlings, of demons, angels and saints...."

"That darling to you, of course, the word darling now, has a lot of resonance. You know if you're interested in that sort of thing, which I don't expect anybody to be except craftsmen and technicians in the trade itself, but, *Charlie is My Darling*, that song *Charlie is My Darling*. It's not just a term of endearment between men and women. It has other resonance. So, darling of angels, demons and saints, and the whole broken-hearted host means that one which is beloved and cherished by the whole, all the inhabitants of the whole cosmos, that is the arisen one. That is the Christ, or that is the Messiah, or that is the Redeemer, that is that highest aspect of one's own being that has the regenerative capacity. But all those, all that kind of explanation is completely irrelevant to the music of a passage which can evoke those things. But as soon as that evocation is clouded or obscured by the kind of mechanism in the heart or the mind that would desire such an explanation, then the song has failed."

"I think *Hey That's No Way to Say Good-bye* is an older song, isn't it? It goes back to your days in Hydra."

"The song was written at the Henry Hudson Hotel on 57th St. in New York City. I think it was begun at...I've just forgotten the name of the hotel in the village, not the Chelsea, it was another hotel where a lot of musicians used to stay — I've just forgotten the name of it. Anyways, it was begun at that hotel and finished at the Henry Hudson, and it was another one of those poems, another one of those songs that were easily and swiftly begun and completed...who lights it, who extinguishes it, and this is not something that is appropriate to words of conversation. It is appropriate to that kind of song, or that kind of expression.

I tried to leave you...

He was now sitting perched, bird-like on his cot.

"The last line of that song was changed by someone. The last line I had somewhat differently, *Hey That's No Way To Say Good-bye.* I met a woman in Toronto at the time, she was working for the CBC, her name was Myra, Moira, and I sang her the song, she liked it very much. And in singing it back to me she changed the melody slightly in the last line and I recognized it immediately as an improvement, so I incorporated it. It happens sometimes. The people you work with or the musicians will slightly modify a song and make it better."

"I wonder if I could just hear the end of that? Can you play it, just..."

"It's hard to get right into it. But I forget what my original version was. It wasn't as helpful to the song as the one I use now."

"It seems suitable for the narrow bed though."

We now moved into the living room, a room it seemed to me to be for the haunted heart.

"*The Story of Isaac*, what's the story of *The Story of Isaac*?"

"*The Story of Isaac*, I don't remember much about that one. As a matter of fact I remember I was writing that at the same time I was living at the Landmark Motel in Los Angeles. As a matter of fact Janis Joplin was living there at the time. I think Bobby Newirth was living there at the time, there were a few people living there. I'd already begun it, I think I began it up here, working on the lyrics, during that period."

"It seems to be both Biblical and personal in a kind of way. I was nine years old, and talking about your father, or a father. Is that in it, do you think?"

"There's that in it. Door opens slowly, my father he came in, I was nine years old. You have to have force of a real emotion, to carry the song through from beginning to end. It's so complex to establish the connection between you and the sacrifice, or your father and Isaac. Who is the sacrifice? I forget that story now. Was it Abraham and Isaac?"

"Abraham and Isaac."

"Isaac is about to be sacrificed."

He seemed reluctant to continue with the thought so we moved on again.

"Simpler I suppose are the couple of songs which you did with Phil Spector. How did that come about?"

"Phil Spector...we had a mutual friend and we were introduced. And I was locked up in his house one evening, I visited him, and he locked the door. Apparently it's his way, he locks the door from the inside so that only he can determine when his guests can leave. And he controls the environment very carefully. You can't turn a light on. And he keeps the place at about fifty degrees so you generally have to wear an overcoat. But I've always loved his work. I loved his songs. I don't know if you remember his songs. *To Know Him is to Love Him* — [sings] He has great songs. All the way from that to *River Deep–Mountain High* with Tina Turner. And certainly the most influential innovator of the music that we call rock music today. A great genius. And I was visiting him one evening and he wouldn't let me out of the house so I said since I've got to be here let's go to work and do something. So we started working on some songs, and we wrote a number of songs very, very swiftly. And one of them was the song I do in the concert called, *Memories*. 'Frankie Lane was singing *Jezebel*.' Frankie Lane was one of my favorite singers, still is. I don't know if you knew that song, *Jezebel*?"

In the concerts Leonard does a musical strip tease on stage. He tosses in enthusiasm and vitality that brings the audience to its feet.

Frankie Laine was singing Jezebel
I pinned an Iron Cross to my lapel
I walked up to the tallest
    and the blondest girl
I said, "Look, you don't know me now
    but very soon you will;
so won't you let me see,
won't you let me see,
won't you let me see your naked body?"

She said, "Just dance me
to the dark side of the gym
Chances are,
    I'll let you do most anything
I know if you're hungry
    I can hear it in your voice
and there are many parts of me to touch
    you have your choice.
But no, you cannot see.
no, you cannot see,
no, you cannot see my naked body."

We're dancing close,
the band is playing Stardust
Balloons and paper streamers
    floating down on us
She says, "You've got a minute left
    to fall in love."
In solemn moments such as this
    I've put my trust
and all my faith to see,
all my faith to see.
all my faith to see her naked body.

I asked him why it was so different. It seems so different than the other songs in the concert. *Iodine* was him as well?

"Yes I did *Iodine*. I stopped doing *Iodine*. We didn't quite have as good a version of it."

"Ah, a couple of older songs that people seem to want to hear over and over again. If you could talk a little, just briefly about *Suzanne*."

"*Suzanne* I wrote in Montreal. I had been working on the melody and the idea. The landscape that was being written out was the landscape around the church Notre Dame de Bonne Secours, which is down the street. That was the feeling in the song, those buildings, the St. Lawrence, Our Lady of the Harbour is Notre Dame de Bonne Secours. And I had the melody, or I had the accompaniment and then an old friend of mine, whose name was Suzanne, invited me down to her place near the river, and she served me tea and oranges that come all the way from China. And you know the purity of the event was not compromised by any carnality and the song is almost reportage. It's just a very accurate evocation of exactly what happened. But the song had begun. It was as though she handed me the seed for the song.

"That's the song and that's the landscape of old Montreal, that is the church. She becomes of course Our Lady of the Harbor. Notre Dame de Bonne Secours, Our Lady of Good Health is her church already there. But Suzanne becomes an incarnation of that church for sailors. That is a church for sailors. Inside the church there are models of ships hanging. That is the church that faces the river, and it is when the sailors are blessed from that church. So the next verse moves easily, you know onto the idea that Jesus was a sailor, sank beneath your wisdom like a stone. So you know you could establish a real coherence in the song if that was where you went, you know if you liked to do those sort of things. But it hangs together very, very neatly."

Suzanne takes you down
to her place by the river
you can hear the boats go by
you can spend the night beside her
And you know that she's half crazy
but that's why you want to be there
and she feeds you tea and oranges
that come all the way from China
And just when you mean to tell her
that you have no love to give her
then she gets you on her wavelength
and she lets the river answer
that you've always been her lover.

> And you want to travel with her
> And you want to travel blind
> And you know that she can trust you
> For you've touched her perfect body
> With your mind.

And Jesus was a sailor
when he walked upon the water
and he spent a long time watching
from his lonely wooden tower
and when he knew for certain
only drowning men could see him
he said All men will be sailors then
until the sea shall free them.
but he himself was broken
long before the sky would open
forsaken, almost human
he sank beneath your wisdom like a stone
> And you want to travel with him

you want to travel blind
and you think maybe you'll trust him
for he's touched your perfect body
with his mind.

Now Suzanne takes you hand
and she leads you to the river
she is wearing rags and feathers
from Salvation Army counters
And the sun pours down like honey
on our lady of the harbor
And she shows you where to look
among the garbage and the flowers.
There are heroes in the seaweed
there are children in the morning
they are leaning out for love
they will lean that way forever
while Suzanne holds the mirror
    And you want to travel with her
    you want to travel blind
    and you know that you can trust her
    for she's touched your perfect body
    with her mind

"But of course you can't take credit for really good songs like that because you begin every song with the intention of writing a good song. Now what is it that allows you to write very well on one occasion and very badly or in a mediocre fashion on another occasion?"

"I wonder whether the city of Montreal and it being a port has anything to do with the background of some of the thoughts passing through. It seems there's a lot of activity of people coming through here, going and coming."

"Well, I think yes. The port has meant a lot. The song *Passing Through* is a song I learned when I was fifteen, from a very devoted socialist that I knew. That particular version of the song comes out of *The People's Song Book* which was a song book developed out of the interest that the socialists had at one time in folk music, still have. It came out of the Almanac Singers, who later became the Weavers, that's the group that Pete Seeger was in — the book was edited by John Lomax. The book itself was very influential in interesting me in song and songwriting. I came across it when I was about fifteen."

"Marianne, was a real person?"

"Yes. I lived with Marianne for a long time. I met her in Greece and we lived together for many years."

"It seems to be one of the most popular of all the old songs. Do you have any thoughts as to why that is?"

"I think it's a good song. It was filled with emotion that was authentic. It fell into place. It's hard to say, you know, why a song works or it doesn't work. But she is a muse, and many writers have written songs for her, this is one of them."

"But you're sort of saying good-bye. You seem to be saying good-bye to a lot of people."

"Yes, well there's a certain kind of writer that says hello to people in their songs and there's a certain kind of writer that says good-bye to people. And you know I'm more of a writer of elegies — how do you pronounce that word?"

"That sounds right."

"Elegies, at least in that particular phase. Well you see, the thing is that I think for many writers the work has a prophetic quality. I don't mean in a cosmic or religious sense, but just in terms of one's own life — you are generally writing about events that haven't taken place yet. Those are the appropriate occasions for song-making, you're generally treating the event. It is such events that have an emotional part. And those are appropriate moments to treat in that kind of expression."

"How about *The Stranger Song*?"

"That's a good song. I wrote *The Stranger Song* over a long period of time but I finished it in the Penn Terminal Hotel on 34th Street in New York City. I'd been writing it in a lot of places here, and Greece and on airplanes. I have a lot of scraps of paper with lyrics of that song written on it.

"Ah, you mention a lot of hotels, and a lot of places in our conversation and on tour, it seems a crazy way to make a living somehow."

"Because there are a lot of hotels. See, when I started to make a living my standard of living deteriorated swiftly. Because before I had any money I was living in a very beautiful house in Greece for about $1100 a year. It was my entire expenses and you have the sunlight and those white rooms and Marianne, a very rich and productive life. Then I started to make money and I found myself living in hotel rooms and spending time in airports and buses, extremely dreary rooms all throughout the world in very bad climates. So that my real standard of living deteriorated considerably when I had money. Well, it's very difficult to give a metaphysical explanation for why you're doing a thing. I suppose I did it because the song seized me – and the appetite for reaching many people seized me."

"And now?"

"In a sense I think that I don't want to make any dramatic statement of renunciation. These statements are usually inaccurate in any case. I feel that there is a new spirit in my work. Maybe beginning with this last batch of songs and that the songs I write will not have that quality, that elegaic quality in them any longer. That there is, there is a new spirit in the songs."

"I found it interesting, one of the songs is titled *The Singer Must Die*."

"'The Singer Must Die for the lie in his voice,' is the whole line. I think that's true. It's hard to look back at a song and try to really discover the aesthetic or the argument of a song. A real song has no argument. But I think one of the things I was trying to say is that you can't fake a song or a poem or a piece of work, or even, what a man is in the world... it withers if it isn't based on, on what is authentic and what is true. In other words, you can lie for a little while, maybe, in what we call art, but that lie tarnishes a piece of work very swiftly. And if it isn't really grounded on real experiences and the real expression of that experience, it's bound to wither. And 'A singer must die for the lie in his voice.'

We moved to several songs that provided surprising answers. Just a couple more of these.

"'Dear Lady, Queen of Solitude, from *Our Lady of Solitude*.' See, I like all the forms that exist. I don't think it's necessary to overthrow the Catholic Church, or to revitalize Jewish institutions, or to radically change the form of things. And it's my pleasure to write to the virgin. I have my own understanding of what *Our Lady of Solitude* is, you know, I can develop a construction of that idea so that I could say what is the most intimate part of the psyche — that we have to stay in contact with. That it does have a female quality. That you have to open a certain passive...you have to affirm your own passivity at certain points in your life to be regenerated or to be renewed in moments of pain or alienation. And that is an approach, an address to that part of the psyche which is silent and which is receptive, and which can only be affirmed by silence and passivity."

"Who are *The Sisters of Mercy*?"

"The Sisters of Mercy were actually two young women that I met during a snow storm in Edmonton, Alberta. And they came to my hotel room and there was something, oh, very agreeable about their company. And they had no place to stay and they fell asleep on my bed, and I stayed up and I remember there was a full moon. And I felt like having something to say to them when they woke up, and that was one of those rare and graceful occasions when I was able to write a song from beginning to end in the space of a few hours. And while they slept I worked on this song. And when they woke up I sang it to them. It was completely full and finished, and they liked it. Barbara and Lorraine were their names."

"It was used by Robert Altman in a film. How did you get involved with Robert Altman? What brought that about?"

"Robert Altman called me. I was recording in Nashville and he located me and he said that he wanted to use the music from my first record in a movie that he was making, called *McCabe and Mrs. Miller*. And that it wasn't just that he wanted some music for the film, but he had written and conceived the film while listening to the record. In a sense these songs were the genesis of the film and he deeply needed them, that they were a part of the film already. So he showed me some rough cuts of the film and, of course I agreed, and that's how it came about."

"Did that change you life? Being a writer of a film?"

"Not in the least, not in the least. Although the film played widely, it wasn't really seized as the little classic that it is until quite a few years later. So that there wasn't really much attention connected to the film."

"I guess part of the poet's function is to ask questions. And one of the songs I like a lot is *Who By Fire*? It seems to be just a series — "

He stopped me.

"'Who by fire? Who by water?' That song derives very directly from a Hebrew prayer that is sung on the Day of Atonement, or the evening of the Day of Atonement. 'Who by fire? Who by sword? Who by water?' There is, according to the tradition, the book of life which is open and in it is inscribed all those who will live and all those who will die for the following year. And in that prayer is catalogued all the various ways in which you can quit this veil of tears. The melody is, if not actually stolen, is certainly derived from the melody that I heard in the synagogue as a boy. But of course the conclusion of the song as I write it is somewhat different. 'Who shall I say is calling?'"

"Who is calling?"

"That is what makes the song into a prayer, for me in my terms, which is, who is it, or what is it that determines who will live and who will die? What is the source of this great furnace of creation? Who lights it? Who extinguishes it?"

In the film I married his lyric to the soulful sound of the Cantor. Even now, every few years in the temple, I pray with Leonard in song.

[Cantor Singing / Mandolin begins]

Who by fire? Who by water? Who in the sunshine? Who in the night time? Who by high ordeal? Who by common trial? Who in your merry, merry month of May? Who by very slow decay? And who shall I say is calling?

Who in her lonely slip? Who by barbiturate? Who in these realms of love? Who by something blunt? Who by avalanche? Who by powder? Who for his greed? Who for his hunger? And who shall I say is calling?

Who by brave ascent? Who by accident? Who in solitude? Who in this mirror? Who by this lady's command? Who by his own hand? Who in mortal chains? Who in power? And who shall I say is calling?

On the tour... I became a traveler to a strange land — the world of the music superstar. Now that I think back on it, the only time I have experienced the crowd in this sense was when I lived briefly in Mexico and attended the Sunday bullfights. The crowd, the mass, the fans cheered for elegance, splendor under danger, and even more they cheered for blood. Leonard's tour took him mostly to sports venues and occasionally majestic concert halls, a journey of exhaustion to the level of pain.

I thought I had planned for everything in advance of the tour.

The camera was new, the film stock checked and double-checked. The camera position studied as if I were a marksman, ready for battle. We even arranged for our own tour bus to join the forces of 'Field Commander Cohen.' We were ready for the singing war. I had planned on everything except Belgium.

Belgium, you ask?

Yes, Belgium. We traveled all night and all day to Antwerp to join Leonard who had already been on the road for days and long nights. He looked like a fighter going on around ten or so. I tried joking with him before the performance at the Koningin Elizabethzaal, an antique hall where you might encounter German *lieder* sung by a overdressed soprano with tightly clasped white-gloved hands or a balding tenor in frayed tuxedo, ironed to the point of vanishing. Yes, Belgium.

Yes, Belgium which is a country, much like a green lawn which has been saturated by chemicals to drown the weeds and all other independent living matter. Every blade in its place. None would dare to be different. Belgium is to countries — what Robert Goulet is to music. Help, please! Belgium is, of course, now the center of the new homogenized Europe where the new bland Euro is the currency and the politicians are selected to be indistinguishable, erasing all signs of rationality. The new world of the neuter and the neutral. Gone are quaint terrible wars that kept Europe constantly off balance. Now the balanced budget and the balanced citizen in a state unknown.

So, we began in our merry, merry way innocently with cameraman Ken Gregg wandering about on stages now focused on the singing of Leonard and then on an audience that seemed dressed for a funeral and behaved the same.

Leonard was obsessed and upset. Foolishly, I tried interviewing him during the stagnant intermission. He spoke with an angry intensity. He was like a passionate lover who had been unfairly rebuked.

"Now, there's certain times, you know, when you are wrong,

and you have to take responsibility for it, but there's certain times when the audience is wrong, and they have to take responsibility for it. They'll be punished severely. I'm not going to let them get away with this. This is the best music that has been played in Belgium, what's the, when was the last Belgian composer? Where's Ava, she knows. Doesn't matter anyways. I want to tell you."

I tried to be judicially calming.

"What's the difference between one audience and another, one down and one up? What's the difference?"

"Search me. You could say it's our fault, you could say it's our fault. We're tired, we've been on the road a long time. Perhaps there's some special element that is missing from our presentation. I don't think so. I think it's the most passionate presentation I've seen in a long time. I'm afraid, that in this case, the people are to blame. The people are to blame. From time to time you have to come to that. These people work hard all week. You know, you can't expect... how excited can they be at ten-thirty? They're used to going to bed at nine or ten, but they never go to bed at ten-thirty."

The band joined in.

"We've got an old and a very well dressed audience tonight which already says a lot."

"What does it say? What does it say?"

"That they are very calm and only applauding. I mean there's not the kind of excitement as we have it in France, with a younger audience. This is what I think."

"They're shy."

Leonard, trying to be fair, offered an idea. "They're, they're good — I'm going to go out into them."

"We had the same problem in Germany a few times."

"Slay 'em Leonard."

"Good. Okay. We're behind you."

"And remember, the race is not always to the swift."

"And when the going gets tough, the tough get going."

"Or the battle to the strong. Nor yet riches to men of understanding. But time and chance happeneth to them all."

[The transcript notes violin music]

After the grueling game of performance the local press came by to ask why he had not included Phil Spector.

Leonard polite, always polite, responded. "We do a couple of them in the concert."

The interviewer persisted. "A couple? I only remember one."

Leonard gently answered.

"I only did one? Well I only did one here because I felt this audience didn't want to be troubled too much by any noise. I think the audience was very gentle and tired and that they didn't want anything too loud."

The interviewer, being very Belgian, compromised. "Probably also because that's what they expect from you. You are a very intimate singer, and Spector is a man of spectacular things. In fact here are two extremes who met, which is very surprising."

Leonard smiled and gave a smiling answer to make light of a heavy situation. "Well, Spector has done some very beautiful and soft tunes like, 'To know, know, know him, is to love, love, love him, and I do... yes I do.' You see, that was when he was in his Debussy phase. But I met him when he was in his Wagnerian phase."

The interviewer wanted to show he had done his reading. "In the new album, you say, on the sleeve, that you were influenced by Persian poets, for instance."

"That's right."

"And also by Chinese people."

"That's right."

"That is for the lyric signs, for the lyrics?"

"For the lyrics, yes. Well, also musically of course, I turned a bit towards the middle east and towards the Eastern European sound using a Russian violinist and an Armenian oud player. There is I think a very Eastern flavor to it."

"And a very Slavic one."

"Slavic, yeah, that's it."

"Is it because you met people from there, or was it something which attracted you?"

"I've always liked that kind of music, and before my mother died she said to me, 'Why don't you play any of those songs that we used to sing?' My mother used to sing me beautiful Russian songs, when I was young. And she said, 'Why don't you get a violin and make songs like the ones we used to sing?' So I think that may have been some influence on it also."

"You still speak Russian today also?"

"No, I've forgotten all my Russian."

"You're a Canadian now."

"Yes."

"You are singing French on the record, also."

"Yeah."

"And in the combination of this French text with ah, rather Mexican tune, is surprising."

"Bizarre, yeah, it's bizarre."

"How did you get that idea?"

"Well I thought that had some interesting resonances.... a Jewish-English-Canadian singing of French independence, independent hymn with a mariachi band from a restaurant in Los Angeles. I thought that had certain interesting harmonics."

"From the lyric point of view again, I find the new album much more complicated, more difficult to understand than for instance in the previous one. It's again poetry which is full of symbols, I have the impression. Is that right?"

"Well I tried to make it as simple as possible."

"I found the first, the previous one much simpler to understand. You are not aware of that?"

"Well, I never try for anything obscure. I try to make it as simple as I can. Sometimes, maybe, I fail, or sometimes it takes a while for the thing itself to become clear. For instance my friend, Harry Rasky, he didn't think my new book *Death of a Lady's Man* was very good. I could tell. Until he lived with it for awhile and the thing becomes clearer. You know? And I think that's a very justifiable position. You know that a piece of work takes some time, you know assuming that the man has done it with a certain amount of seriousness and you're not just trying to fool or deceive anyone, but assuming that you've worked with a serious purpose, I think it's quite understandable that a piece of work can take years and years to penetrate the consciousness of the public and to mean something to them. There's nobody to blame, neither the artist nor the public, but sometimes it takes a while for a piece of work to mature, in the public's heart."

"And in the maker's heart, let's say, is there not a moment where you see that certain things do not mature, or are not so good as you planned them?"

"Yes, there's also that other side of the thing where, perhaps, something that you thought held a certain kind of value that it didn't have. But, that happens more rarely than the other thing."

"Yeah?"

"Yeah, because I'm very careful about the work I put out."

"You are a poet in the first place? Or a singer?"

"Well, I don't...you know...that's a verdict that other people can give. Some people will never think I'm a singer and some people will never think I'm a poet. I'm not trying to ... for myself I don't, have, it's not important to me to describe myself. You know, I have some work to do in the world and I try to do it the best I can, and if I can find a public that is receptive to it I'm happy. And if I can't, then I'll still continue doing it."

"You also produced the purely musical side of the album. It means you took care of the arrangements which I think are very nice. The women's voices are very nicely used."

"Yes, well, all those women's voices are Jennifer Warnes. She's not here right now. She was here a second ago, she's in the dressing room. And she overdubbed her voice many times and I kind of combined them but you could say that she's responsible for those arrangements. And you know when you're working with the kind of excellent musicians that I'm working with it's also difficult to take full responsibility for an arrangement. For instance, I didn't arrange the part that John Bilezikjian played. He heard the melody and he added the kind of touch that he would add, or with Raffi Hakopian the violinist, or the organ player. You know, so what it is to gather together very, very good musicians and to present them with a vehicle with which they themselves can express themselves and, in a certain way it arranges themselves. You have a kind of veto on it, but when you are working with this caliber of musician you can't really take full responsibility for the arrangement."

"You've been on the road for some time now. You stopped at a certain moment and now you are back at it again."

"Yeah, this is our eighth or ninth concert on a tour of fifty concerts...fifty-two concerts."

"And it is how long has it been since you did some touring? It must be one or two years, no?"

"It's close to four years."

"Close to four years?"

"Three and a half years."

"And why did you stop?"

"Well, I don't know. I tour rarely, you know. I don't really tour all the time. I'm..."

"You don't like to be on stage? Or, or what?"

"It's not a matter of not liking to be on stage. I don't like to be on stage unless I have something to say. You know, just to get go round the world gathering applause and money it's not a bad idea but it's not really what I'm after. There is a certain moment in your working life when know you got a song, a few songs, a record, a book. The moment arrives when you want to present the work."

"The new album opens with *The Guests*. Is that the most powerful track? Does that mean that it is the song which is the strongest, which attracts the public?"

"It seems to be a well received song. I started the album with it, firstly because the people I played the album for were enthusiastic about that track, but also it defines the album. You see the guests arrive and then the rest of the album is each of the guests makes a statement about his own particular position. And that goes right down through the record to the next side, right down to the end. It's as if each guest tells his story. But it's not necessary to know that about the album. Of course each song stands by itself, but it's unified that way."

"And it's very often about love, and love which is not very happy? Is that your personal approach to it, your personal view on love?"

"Well, it's not, that's not my impression about the album, that it's about unhappy love."

"No?"

"I feel it's about deep and fulfilled love and about the mechanics of love, but not about the disappointments specifically, about the whole landscape."

"There is the second song which is, if I recall well, *Humbled Love*?"

"Um hmm."

"Which I think is rather my favorite song, and is it true that there is some irony in it? Or am I wrong?"

"There's some good lyrics in it. You see, I mean that's a song, humbled."

And so — into the night. Gently, politely. Leonard fielded question after question. I drank the brandy.

It was the only time that he and I would have a moment of misunderstanding. He had been deeply hurt and troubled by his

Belgian waffle reception.

He suggested that, perhaps, it was the presence of the camera that distracted the audience. Was the film really a good idea?

There is always a moment of truth between subject and creator of a personal film. It is a kind of challenge. And I took it.

Okay, I indicated that if I could not make, our crew invisible I would leave. We agreed. That's when I sent for Jean Reitberger, a diminutive, almost invisible cameraman, with whom I had worked in Ethiopia, making the *Lion and the Cross* for CBS. Jean was based in France. He would join my film-making force and we would vanish by mounting the cameras behind black curtains, from both sides of the stage, while I called out silent directions on a walkie-talkie.

Invisible we became as we moved on to France.

Of course, Montpellier and Leonard seemed made for each other. It's a university town, as they used to say in dispatchers, "Somewhere in France." We had to fly from Antwerp, so it's exact location remains a mystery. But it is a university town and the young people and Leonard seemed a single unit. There was no generation gap and they had come to the Palais de Sports to just let go. And Leonard felt the same way after the repression of Belgium — free at last.

After that there was no further discussion about the film crew being in the way. We were in harmony. Leonard was glowing. He seemed to rise up from the brilliance of the powerful lights. His very stillness had its own poetry. Magic. He was making a sentimental journey into the soul. Nightmagic.

Here he was wooer of emotions, now the ageless lover. And truly the women went moist and the men could only observe with a kind of benevolent envy. But anyone who could turn language into lust deserved their bravos, of which there were many.

And after the draining performance the inevitable backstage interviews. Here is part of a transcript:

"Would you accept the image of being called a loner?"

He sang a little mockingly and skipped the light fantastic.

"Sometimes alone, sometimes, you know, sometimes happy, sometimes blue, that I ran into you."

"You don't live up to images?"

"Frankly, images are something other people make for themselves, it's just a kind of lie, a kind of way of making your way through the world. Everybody has one, whether it's the public one or just among your friends and acquaintances everybody has a kind of image."

Now, a little philosophy.

"And what about, there's an

Austrian poet, I'd like to quote him, he's been saying the real adventures are in your head, and if they're not in your head, they aren't anywhere. Where do your adventures take place?"

Heavy stuff, for a post concert conversation but Leonard, as always, was game.

"Well, you know, you can't ever criticize a poet, but, what he says is only half true, I mean there are the adventures in your head, but there are also the physical adventures, and the real adventures in life, and there is a real world, and we really are in the real world. We have our bodies, and there's real adventures. There's real mountains, there's real houses, there's real women, there's real problems, there's real adventures as well as the ones in your head."

The pop culture press is its own unique brand of journalism. The recent rating of a song is cause for probing.

"Tonight you seem to have more, to be more...well...outward, doing these particular songs. One time you didn't seem to like your audience, your former audience?"

"Yeah, I didn't like it myself, and most of my audience didn't like it. I received a lot of letters saying that they thought I had betrayed them. But, ah, I think the songs are good, and the record gets better with years, and it starts to sound a lot better to me, now. Maybe Phil had the right idea. I used to think that he had, you know, lost me in the record, lost my voice. But I think he had some good ideas. I think our arrangement is better than his thoughts."

"Let's come back to this image, and fan followers like, you just said they felt betrayed. Do you really sort of plan to fulfill the expectations in some way or other, or do you just try to make your own thing, do your own thing, do your own music the way you like it, and...?"

"Well, I think you do both, it's, you know, it's, it's pleasant to be accepted. It's also important to go your own way, if you can make some kind of harmony between what is expected of you and what you expect from yourself, that's a good way to go."

"Okay."

The polite European seemed satisfied. Now came a young woman representing Canada, anxious to prove points, no doubt, convinced she could do it better.

"You've been called by some German papers, 'a poet of rock music.' Whatever you do I don't call it rock music, how would you characterize yourself?"

Leonard braced himself, always a gentleman.

"Well, I think that's some title they gave to me about twelve years ago. I think by rock music, we meant at that particular time, the kind of music that spoke directly from the heart, directly from the body, directly from the soul as opposed to the kind of artificial music that was going on at the time. Nowadays rock music as a description doesn't really mean very much, and as for myself being a poet or not, that's something other people have to decide."

Still poking, prodding, punching really.

"And how would you call yourself?"

Leonard was wonderful.

"Well, I, you know, when I wake up in the morning I don't call myself anything. I just brush my teeth and wash my face, and try to start the day, like when you wake up you don't call yourself a journalist."

"Well, if, you stay at night in a hotel and you have to sign in, what do you sign in for profession?"

"Oh well, if I have to sign in I say writer, or farmer, or something, I mean, you know..."

"Would you think you express yourself much better in music than in lyrics. I mean the written lyrics."

"Well, I try to do my best in each of the forms, you know sometimes I blow it, sometimes I blow in song, sometimes I blow it in writing. Sometimes I succeed in a song, sometimes I succeed in the writing."

"And if you look at it, look back from the last years do you feel more success in music, or more success in writing?"

"In my own heart I don't separate it."

"You don't separate it?"

"I don't separate it."

"You said again, before, on the stage sometimes you are happy and sometimes blue, but when I watched you tonight I felt you much more blue than happy. I can never really see you really smile."

"Oh well, you know, I felt pretty good. Some people when they feel good, they just look sad. You know some people have what you might call a melancholy eye."

"You don't come to that?"

"Sort of, I, think I got that from my mother. She felt best when she felt blue. You know, some people like to feel a little blue. We like to feel we've been down and sad, and looking over things. You know that's not quite the same as, as being unhappy."

"When I prepared for tonight I had a look in my library, and I found some funny, expressions there. Some called you 'the second Bob Dylan.' Somebody else thought about a 'competitor of Bob Dylan,' and somebody said about like a 'secret twin of Bob Dylan.' Did you ever feel to be compared to Bob Dylan. Or do you like to be compared with anybody?"

Always generous, Leonard wanted to set things right.

"I feel that Bob Dylan is my brother. I feel we are doing the same thing. Ah, I feel he does it a little better than I do it. Most of the time. Sometimes I feel I do it a little better than he does it. But there's no competition between me and Bob Dylan. Bob Dylan, has a huge worldwide audience. I have a tiny audience. I'm just a kind of corner singer. I just sing in some corners."

"Well, it didn't seem to me a corner tonight, out there."

"Well, these people are from the corner too, you know. This is not a huge stadium of 25,000 people, it's still quite a small hall. And these are people that I feel know my work and have known it for some years and they recognized the music and they've come because the music has already touched them."

"In 1973 you left and you said you'd never come back again on stage."

"I did?"

"Did you?"

"I don't know."

"You probably forget, or did I read something wrong, I don't know."

"I don't know, but you know, you can't believe everything you read. But I, well, I haven't been back for a while, I mean, I'm very careful to not overstay my welcome. I think it was three and a half to four years before, since I've been here."

In your book, which I think in English you call the *Favorite Game*...it's very self-biographic isn't it? It has some touch of it anyhow?"

"Yeah, there's things from my childhood."

"And there's a lot of irony in it, but in your songs I don't feel the same irony, I think there's something different in your songs than in the book. Do I feel wrong or right about that?"

"Well, I've got to tell you frankly, it's hard for me to say what's in them, in the songs, you know, because I forget who I am most of the time when I'm singing. I don't know what they sound like. You know, that's the one thing I can't tell you about is what I sound like when I sing."

"Do you think the music backs more the idea of war than it may back the idea of peace?"

"Well, you know, I don't think anybody is going to march off to war to my music."

"It's very hard to march in a tango rhythm, or in a slow waltz. There's no doubt about that. It would look funny if they would march or tango to the waltz."

"If you are going to speak in those terms I would say that, if you were going to talk about the political aspect of my music I would say that it's the music of personal resistance."

Enough. Enough. Sleep would be welcome.

I had watched Leonard be accused of all forms of flaw. But the audience had caressed him, even protected him.

He looked both powerful and vulnerable, if that is possible, desperately in need of care, yet able to be the caretaker of all frail souls. He had exposed every emotion and they loved him.

Next morning, at dawn, we were at the airport wounded by the high of the night before. Leonard and the band slept stretched out on the hard, indifferent airport plastic benches, the pounding of the music of the performance somehow tangled with the jet roar.

Give us this day a little peace and rest!

Not quite. On to Paris and the enthusiasm of another giving audience at the Theatre de Champs Elysees. A mix of sophistication and raw passion. Leonard was armed with the knowledge that his inspiring song *The Guests* had risen to a top spot on the charts.

Leonard himself said he found it strange to have essentially a religious song based on a thirteenth century Persian poem become a number one song. And so, he led off his concert in Paris with *The Guests*.

Let all my guests come in
And no one knows where the night is going
And no one know why the wine is flowing
Love, I need you, I need you, I need you, I need you.

And all go stumbling through that house
In lonely secrecy
Saying, Do reveal yourself
Or, Why hast thou forsaken me

And no one knows where the night is going
And no one know why the wine is flowing
O love, I need you, I need you, I need you now.

All at once the torches flare
The inner door flies open
One by one they enter there
In every style of passion

And no one knows where the night is going
And no one knows why the wine is flowing
O love, I need you, I need you
I need you, I need you now

Next stop Germany.

In Germany Leonard is considered the voice of conciliation, as well as love. Here the audience understands him as someone who understands them.

Here, too, I feel Leonard and I bonded. Here he offered himself in a truly brotherly way. He invited me to share his bus. I took my crew aboard and some of his crew rode in our much more humble vehicle.

Here I asked him about his own attitude — a Jew, singing before a German audience in post–holocaust Germany — one song in particular. How does he feel? How do they feel?

"Leonard...your first concert in Germany, and when you did your television show, what was it you said to the audience about *The Partisan Song*?"

"Ah, I said this song concerns the activities of your great grandfathers, vis-à-vis my great-grandfathers. And, ah, I said that the connection between you and your great-grandfathers is very tenuous, whereas the connection between me and my great-grandfathers is continuous. And that this makes for a certain resonance in the song."

"Do you have any sense — Leonard Cohen is a wonderful Jewish name — that there's any kind of strange feeling in Germany?"

"The first time I came to Germany, which was about ten years ago, to sing and I was very much aware of the history of this country in relation to the history of my own people. So naturally, one had all the reservations, justifiable paranoia, suspicion, resentment. But the hospitality of the audiences was such that that soon dissolved. And now I'm always happy to be in Germany."

"I was thinking of an article I read about Isaac Stern that said he couldn't perform in Germany, but on the other hand he thought that young Israelis should perform in Germany because he thought that the generations were so different. Do you have that same kind of feeling?"

"To tell you the truth I find all these discussions of Jews in relation to Germany very, very spurious and, they really don't touch my heart. The whole idea of music is to dissolve these all too human prejudices and concerns. You know, so what if people are at each others throats the next morning. The point is that in the midst of the song they're not. And that's what the song's for. And to mix up all of these things seems to me to be really unnecessarily complicating the process of music. You know, far more important, if you do have these concerns to understand that at a certain moment during a song there is no difference between anybody in that hall. If the song is true and powerful, at that moment when it is being sung and when it is being listened to, there are no Germans and there are no Jews. That's what music is for...?

I tried to interrupt.

"Do you have —"

"I get really angry about these questions about Jews and Germans. You can't live your life on the barricades like that. You know, you can on a certain personal level, if you have a deep conviction, and you've got to consecrate your life to hating Germans, or to saving refugees. Both those things are, I suppose, valid in their own world, but there has to be another world, an absolute world, where these distinctions, rather than emphasizing them, generation after generation."

"I think one of the reasons I ask is that looking at the audience and how incredibly enthusiastic they are. I just wondered if there is something in Germany that your words and music turns them on so much. There's a very powerful vibration, I thought. Just sitting at the concert last night, and we're on our way to another one now, whether it had anything to do with nationality or any thing? That's I think the reason..."

"I think that all these antinomies, all these polarities, are embraced. The more difficult, more reconcilable they appear to be, the more stunning is the relief when they dissolve." The more, the more, satisfying it is when these artificial really...when you consider the fact that our little journey on the crust of this star has a number of ridges, barriers, fences, differentiations, diversions that we mange to construct for ourselves to have an opportunity to dissolve them is really a great opportunity. And to carry those distinctions into that moment is a great mistake because that moment is precisely there to dissolve the distinctions. You can't live a life where the distinction are dissolved. We need our distinctions and we need to follow who we are and to understand what our own heritage and what our own conditioning is. But to live totally in that life of the particular is a great mistake and results in a great deal of suffering. If you don't have the moments when the distinctions are dissolved, then you become a very narrow, prejudiced, dogmatic kind of individual, like I am most of the time. But from time to time I'm, I'm permitted to dissolve these things."

"When you're there with the guitar on that stage that is the moment when you're most complete in a kind of way..."

"That's the moment when I am most no one and so everyone can be mostly no one. And it's in these moments when we're one that we understand what the real fellowship is which politicians only seem to arrive at when they're talking about race and blood and soil. And we know what results from those kind of expressions. People can be made to dissolve their differences by very different means and it's important to understand the difference between an artist and a theologian, or a politician. To me an artist does not have a platform, does not have a message, does not have a party. His only message, his only part is the dissolution of differences. And we have to leave it to these other kinds of experts to get us all inflamed about one particular view or another. But in the moment of a song or a poem or an embrace between a man or a woman, or a handshake, between two people, in that moment things are dissolved, and that's the artist's realm."

I thought his thought was beautifully stated, as articulate as one of his poems.

"One last thing. I noticed you don't sing that beautiful song, the French Canadian song that you did with the mariachis, about the wandering Canadian which always haunts me. Is there any reasons why... just curious?"

"Yes, well the original version of the song as we recorded it was just spontaneous. I happen to meet with a group of mariachi players, and I had the idea of this curious song by an English-speaking Jew exiled from Montreal, in Los Angeles with Mexican musicians. So it had curious harmonics and resonances. We cannot play that music authentically, although I'm with probably with the finest musicians in America today. They don't happen to be Mexican mariachi players and for us to simulate the sound is something, we don't do naturally. So we've been working on another version of the song and probably will get around to it."

We joined on board the bus now, Leonard and the whole group and I were invited along in a hummed hymn to understanding as we pulled into the Jahrhunderthalle, a giant stadium in Frankfurt, my last stop.

He would continue to thirty or forty cities, anxious but always giving with the attitude that giving is living.

And that was genuine weeping for sorrow as he closed the concert with a ballad of departing and changing love.

I loved you in the morning
Our kisses deep and warm
Your hair upon the pillow
Like a sleepy golden storm
Many loved before us
I know that we are not new
In city and in forest
They smiled like me and you
But now it's come to distances
And both of us must try
Your eyes are soft with sorrow
Hey, that's no way to say goodbye

I'm not looking for another
As I wander in my time
Walk me to the corner
Our steps will always rhyme
You know my love goes with you
As your love stays with me
It's just the way it changes
Like the shoreline and the sea
But it's not talk of love or chains
And things we can't untie
Your eyes are soft with sorrow
Hey, that's no way to say goodbye

I loved you in the morning
Our kisses deep and warm
Your hair upon the pillow
Like a sleepy golden storm

Yes many loved before us
I know that we are not new
In city and in forest
They smiled like me and you.
But let's not talk of love and chains
And things we can't untie,
Your eyes are soft with sorrow
Hey, that's no way to say goodbye

It certainly was no way to say good-bye — at least for me. I was truly feeling sorrow for the concerts I would not participate in. At best, I was a temporary fellow traveler in this embrace of love.

Reality came brutally.

That night I stayed up late at the indifferent German hotel. I could not sleep with the echo and the shadow of the echo of all these love ballads stunning my brain, truly a vivid, voluptuous torture. I decided to go down to the indifferent bar where raucous, pot-bellied, German businessmen in loud voices foamed with their oversize beer mugs. Here the Germans with gray hair and flushed-red faces who would have been of military age during World War II toasted the night away, now salesmen of the new prosperous Germany. I shivered a little, having made some holocaust films, and in my head I heard other music — march music. I was cursed with a vivid imagination. Sometimes a blessing, but not now with the beer flowing. They caught sight of my bearded face and turned away from me, turning back to what memory?

It was impossible to take a night stroll because the cinder-block hotel stood painfully isolated on a main highway. Just as I was about to head back to my closet-sized room, Leonard appeared, looking, extra lean, sporting a handsome German girl, a *fraulein* of the night, perhaps his 'femme de jour.'

Life on the road is a bitch. Bright lights, bruising sound. Night after night after night. A melange of countries — an assortment of cities and dreams of home. So, for the band there was always 'toys for the boys,' blonde or brunette, many a girlish giggle and souvenirs to bring back to classmates. For Leonard who was a man in musical mourning for his wife and life, there was a more serious standard. Old friends, old tours remembered. But someone always there, if he desired, and for the women, a memoir of "my night with Leonard Cohen." I have noted that these sleepy-eyed ladies never welcomed intruders. They seemed to have a smothering, mothering desire to turn the bird on the wire into the bird in the cage.

So, when Leonard suggested "Harry, why don't you join us for a hamburger?" Greta or Helga or whatever her name was greeted me with a nocturnal, unwelcoming glare.

Now, you must picture the night —Hitchcock with schnitzel. The all-consuming fog hung over everything. To put your face out the door of the faceless hotel was to bathe in particles of dusty moisture and matter. The hotel bar served no food more serious than pretzels and peanuts and the drunken possible former S.S. guards had consumed them all.

Greta or Helga said there was an all-night roadside restaurant twenty or thirty kilometers down the road. And so we climbed into Greta's luxurious, dark-green Mercedes, I was dumped into the back. Anywhere you travel in Germany is also a trip into the past. And the past seemed to consume our voyage to hamburgers on the Hitler-built autobahn. Lead kindly light! My mind was somewhere in the early forties. Messershmidts danced in my head. *Achtung!*

We arrived at a plastic Brecht-like restaurant, too indifferent to be a sad café. It was Burger King with soiled checkered tablecloths. Half-full of formless German businessmen who looked identical to the ones we left behind at the bar. The headwaiter arrived, obviously demoted from some fancier establishment, as

Greta-Helga told him we were after nocturnal hamburgers. He responded he had only goulash. Too late for hamburgers, we decided to stay. We had no other choice.

After a long wait the syrupy goulash was served. Just as I dipped my too-heavy spoon into the brown-gray mush, all the doors of this dark place were flung open and bright lights shone in our faces. There was the sound of boots as soldiers with machine-guns filled the room. Havoc in hamburger heaven! A living nightmare in the night.

Well, well, what have we here?

A young soldier with a metal helmet pulled over his ears and icy blue eyes poked his machine gun in my face.

"Passport!" he demanded.

Every awful World War II film passed before my tired eyes. Suddenly, I was full of unreasonable energy. My Jewish genes had seen enough. This was one Jew they would not take as a surrendering victim.

The young punk in uniform thrust the machine gun closer to my nose and demanded with the authority of the state again: "Passport! Passport!"

I turned with foolish courage, dipped my clumsy spoon into the sour soup and calmly said: "No passport...Goulash." I think I even held it up so he would see it.

Trouble. Stupid trouble. My own deprived, chicken-plucking childhood has never made it comfortable for me to face authority. Sometimes I became the terrified kid with holes in his depression-era socks and now with Leonard Cohen lyrics bruising my sleepless brain, totally, unreasonably confrontational, make of this what you will.

Leonard was stunned by my stupid arrogance. "Harry, what are you doing? Tomorrow you're back in Canada. I've got forty more concerts. I can't afford to spend the night in jail."

Greta-Helga looked at me sarcastically as if to say, 'I knew we should not have brought him.'

A senior officer saw the scene and came over to calm things down. I told him that in free Canada and America we do not carry passports every time we go out for a night-time snack. No passport. He seemed quite reasonable when we explained who we were and he recognized Leonard. In my case, he said he would settle for any form of identification. I had with me an Ontario birth certificate. Naturally it carried no identifying photo. But he was happy to be rid of us.

Greta-Helga acted as translator. "Who were they looking for?"

"Everyone!" The guard said.

In detail, he explained that they had heard that members of the Bader-Meinhof gang were thought to be travelling the autobahn at night. They were not found. The bright lights were dimmed and the normal loud buzz of the business resumed. Needless-to-say not much goulash was consumed by us that night.

Greta-Helga returned us to our hotel with silent disgust in her eyes. Our Jewish eyes were smiling. Leonard embraced me as we parted. What a time! His concert went on and I returned to Canada certain that we had, as they say, the makings of a really good film in the can. And a story to remember:

'First we take Manhattan and then we take Berlin.'

A couple months later I revisited Leonard in Montreal.

He gave me a fellow road-warrior's greeting.

"The tour is over now. What pleased you the most about it?" I asked.

"The fact that it's over is extremely pleasing. Cause it was a difficult tour and parts of it were very badly organized and the musicians and the crew were subjected to a lot of unnecessary travelling and ordeal."

"You have one trophy from it I noticed."

"Well the only thing I brought back was a lovely thing. It's called a...it was from the Odeon Theatre in Edinburgh which is given to those artists that sell out the house. And it's a nice little plaque."

How many plaques and how many cities Leonard has visited since that tour I am not sure. He signed a large poster of himself from a German city, which I treasure. On it he remarked, "for Harry who studies me while I study him."

And so it has been ever since.

As for the film that came from this adventure, I spent months with the consummate film editor Paul Nicholich. My directorial comments were contained on one sheet of paper which I have kept.

HARRY RASKY'S FILM
"THE SONG OF LEONARD COHEN"

Leonard Cohen is the city. He is the French and English Canadian. He is the searching youth. He is the confused Canadian. He is the voice of loneliness. He is religion. He is a lyric. He is a sound. He is the wandering Jew. He is many things. And the film must reflect this. The interweaving of his many meanings is the key to the total effect. The film is a symphony of his sounds and our visualization of what we feel those sounds mean. In telling his story we should be able to tell a lot about ourselves.

The basic device is to use his concert tour as a metaphor for his life and for the aspirations of Canadians generally — pulled apart, dislocated, holding on to old values, experimenting with new ones. His locale is Montreal ... his locale is also the search.. the search for each other... the search for ourselves.

We blend back and forth from song, to interview, to concert — dissolving through to the meaning of lyrics. So, in that sense the film is both a concert and a poetic visualization of the concert... with passages of Cohen talking and reciting. Eventually these talk periods blend with the sounds overlaid by Cohen on the guitar. The entire film is then like a minstrel-commentary on a life and on our times.

And so it is.

The Canadian critics with some notable exceptions dismissed it as Leonard Cohen carrying on and his obsession with women. They just don't get it.

Leonard himself, in the middle of recordings and other singer-chores, saw an almost finished version of the film and expressed a guarded satisfaction. But I knew I had achieved a kind of mystical, musical perfection with the work, or so I felt.

It just felt right. I knew because there was no possible chance — each part blending with the other. I like to describe the making of such a creature as being like the assembly of a great jigsaw puzzle. There can be only one perfect answer to a life or landscape at one given moment and this was it. So the film became like an intricate poem both for the eye and ear. This is neither an expression of ego nor vanity, but the observation of a hard-working craftsman.

Art happens in the head of the creator, sometimes when he is totally unaware of it — great lamentation or great happiness may trigger it — in the hours of sleep or just a surprise in the midst of contemplation. It's part of a vivid wish to hold on to a special moment of emotion, a feeling that can only somehow be released by an act of creation!

In the case of this film being soaked in the blasting colors and exploding sounds, first on the road on tour, and there in the meticulous editing stages, wounded me in a way, left a permanent scar and I was with Leonard bride and groom; we were strivers of a longing to create. I think the film was such a defining experience. At the time, I suppose, I was just dancing on the rooftop of his life — like a drunken green-faced Chagall rabbi with violin. But later, as time passed, I found we had moved into each other's being — trapped. We were bonded brothers.

So when there were meetings, not too many words had to be said. I was having trouble after the film was finished. I had gotten involved in a troubling film called *Being Different*, about freaks. It was about people with physical handicaps, no legs, no arms, an elephant man, midgets, giants, the bearded kid, the alligator man, just name it. And although I tried to mold it in good taste, I still questioned my taste in taking it on. My book, *Nobody Swings on Sunday*, was just out. I acted as host for an entire week of radio on the CBC, on my then-beloved Africa. I was ready to crash and I suppose I did in a way.

I called Leonard in an act of desperation. He responded generously with an immediate invitation to come out to "Camp Cohen," a Buddhist retreat on top of mount Baldy, near Los Angeles. Leonard found solace and satisfaction in this surrounding. I was suitably robed in black, asked to sit straight on a hard bench, fed from a tin bowl, asked to rise at four a.m. to "meditate." Hell, four is when I normally begin sleeping.

Leonard's teacher, master, guru, studied me, tweaked my nose and analyzed, quite correctly, "too much ego." The tweaking brought a sigh of envy from some of the other "patients."

No, no. I decided this was no place for a nice Jewish boy in need of "R & R." I put it precisely to Leonard after a couple days: "Leonard take me down from this mountain or I will walk — please!"

I was not a fit subject for the regions of this mountaintop existence. Leonard with his strange love of the military cherished it! Make of that what you will. I could not see stiffly reciting Sanskrit prayers while the sun was shining — that's where God was for me — in the sunbeam through the green leaves and the birds bathed in God's mystery. Save me, I cried.

Leonard, always understanding, broke away long enough to lower me from the mountain. He admitted that it was at such a moment he had decided to marry a totally inappropriate wife, the gypsy wife of the sad ballad. Perhaps slowly he married her, but it was here he had been overwhelmed by her in his mind. Down in good old decadent Beverly Hills I begged my friends Betty and Sam Jaffe for lodging. Sam, the ancient sage of *Lost Horizon* offered me wisdom and peace of mind. And Leonard sang for him and I was saved, truly saved. Thank you Leonard for attempted solace.

Then the New York evening of the prayer show...

It had become my habit during this period to stay at the Algonquin Hotel on 44th street. The Algonquin had become its own legend. Once it was the home to the powerful players of Broadway. Here Dorothy Parker had quipped her way to fame — "Men never make passes at girls with glasses," etc. At this time, somewhat seedier, home to those wanting a caress from the shadow of the past. There was little humor left except for some of the more portly bellmen. But the Algonquin was the Algonquin.

As I walked into the lobby my assistant cameraman, Johnny Maxwell, still sounding as if he had just landed from Glasgow, lighted up with the greeting, "He's here. The bird on the wire." This was his way of saying, Leonard was at the hotel. We made contact. Contact with Leonard was and is if you have just rejoined part of your being — a missing part of your spirit suddenly found and re-attached.

I went to his room, presuming to have a drink and catch up on a couple years of wandering. We were both wandering Jews. He, more than I.

"I just arrived from Europe, Harry," he said, "*Tvillin* together." *Tvillin* are objects Orthodox Jews attach to the arm, close to the heart and the head, close to the brain, to join God each morning in prayer.

He opened his old-fashioned leather bag which was sparse with clothing and in it were two sets of prayer equipment, shawls and *tvillin*. Why two sets? He never explained. Carefully, I adjusted the binding straps — just the right number as, specified to every pre-bar-mitzvah boy. Leonard was better at it than I. But it gave me a kind of peace. I could recall Tennessee Williams once saying, "Prayer is an act of solace. God is a good word — a short one."

So, here we were two middle-aged traveling Jews, bound together by our past, our film, our prayers, in a tiny room at the Algonquin. Somehow it made perfect sense in a world that seemed to make little sense.

Shma Yisroel, Adonai Elohaynu, Adonai Echod. "Here O'Israel, Lord is our God, the Lord is one."

The Hebrew scholar, Leo Baeck, explained the whole Hebrew idea of prayer in an essay on the essence of Judaism. "As the ancient Hebrew morning prayer says, man 'unifies God' through his love for him. In this desire to 'unify God,' man's creative impulse finds a powerful means of self-expression." The scholar Abraham Joshua Heschel added: "Worship is a way of living, a way of seeing the world in the light of God."

Leonard was striving to find such a light, such a unity. Like other great love poets before him he moved his interest from women and human love to the love of God.

John Donne, one of the masters of female adulation ("Close thy mouth and let me love") graduated — if that is a correct word for it — to Bishop of St. Paul's — a truly buxom beauty. For Leonard it was more time at his mountain retreat searching for the Buddha within him. He wrote a book of poems of worship. He was changing, striving wanting to find unanswerable answers. His music also matured to new heights of spiritual splendor.

He was, and still is in many ways the poet of the broken-hearted and the broken dream, always true to himself, picking up clues from the great poets of the past, such as Robbie Burns who, summed up the ache of the human heart — "Had we never met, and never parted — we n'er would be broken-hearted." Weep for us all — Leonard has tried to do that for us.

All this makes one shudder, especially when you consider the stupidity of so many "music writers" or critics in Canada who insist on reviewing the Leonard of today as they would the Cohen of thirty years age — with suitable juvenile sarcasm.

The Globe & Mail devoted two pages to an event recently — a convention of Cohen admirers held in Montreal. It began, "Imagine a *Star Trek* convention populated entirely by devotees of Sylvia Plath."

The paper was critical of what Cohen's representative wore, critical of the gifts he sent as he could not be there, critical of the new poems he sent.

And sometimes when the night is slow
the wretched and the meek.
Gather up our hearts and go
A thousand kisses deep.

Meanwhile, as Cohen continues his search and evolves into a spirit of the ages, others have given way, given in to other Gods. Bob Dylan sat like a sad-eyed scarecrow at the Kennedy Center honors, now part of the institutions of the century. Author David Brooks, describes a new world, not changing in a book, *Bobos in Paradise: The New Upper Class and How They Got There.* Bob Dylan and Crosby, Stills, and Nash now play concerti at private conferences hosted by Nomura Securities. The bohemians have become bankers. What greater victory can you ask for?

The greatest victory? The greatest victory is still the victory of the heart, the *Neshumah*, the spirit, the soul. Yes. Yes. Yes!

So, when Leonard's call came not so long ago, I was delighted, but somehow not surprised. No pretence! Two old friends touching across the continent.

The fact about Leonard is that despite what some critics do not understand when they say he is always the same, he is always different. A singer-poet is not just a singer. He is full of surprise, always trying to replenish himself with new forms. To some he may seem to be as repetitive as the Bolero, but it is simply not so.

The skilled film giant Robert Altman, crafted a film *McCabe and Mrs. Miller*. Droning away like the mountain snows of British Columbia, Leonard provided the eternal lament. My last major film, *Prophecy*, came to me became of a Leonard lyric. Not long ago I was able to craft it around a fairly recent song, *The Future* and it was totally full of surprises. Leonard somehow manages to be ahead of the headlines. In a time when O.J. walks free, George W. seems to enjoy "frying" the black population of Texas, the air and water we consume has turned to poison, Leonard has proclaimed he's seen the future — and it is murder. And yet, and yet in his weeping for us he still reassures us that the soul is gentle. Leonard, I hope you are right.

In his call to me Leonard said, "Yes, I've come down from the mountain. I feel like a great weight has been lifted." He joked about having found the perfect hotel room.

But then having announced his victory I searched for the searcher and he was gone again — returned to India to the great 'perhaps.'

Many have tried to analyze him, with little success. He eludes you. A quarter century ago the music writer Paul Williams wrote in *Crawdaddy*:

> Talking with Leonard Cohen is like touching the earth unexpectedly after months of subway stations and supermarkets. There's a resiliency in the man and his sense of himself – he seems to know what he is doing. Most contemporary singer-songwriters are not mature artists; they're too young or they tasted success too young and never got past its confusions. Cohen is an exception...
>
> Here is the first of the rock generation to reach maturity with his consciousness and courage and sense of humor intact.

Trying to find the real Leonard has become a kind of favorite game. In a course I taught at the University of Toronto called "The Passionate Canadians," there was much discussion in essays about the real Cohen. Perhaps the most brilliant of the students searched into her own past in art history to recall a work called "Portrait of Ginerva de Benci," by Leonard's namesake, Leonardo DaVinci, the only painting by him in North America. Leonardo had written on the back, "Beauty Adorns Virtue." She speculates that the phrase has stayed with her because it gives reassurance in moments of doubt, when the truth escapes us and we need a reminder of what it is to have learned and observed of humanity. Leonard the searcher for the idea opens up deep hidden depths of why we hurt, why we love.

There is the often quoted maxim of Pascal that "the heart has its reasons, which reason does not know." Cohen's out-cry is this terror we live with in the battle between our heart and our head, and from that, a craving to understand. Even Dr. James Watson, discoverer of the double helix and a profound atheist, had to admit to me that the gene for love will probably never be found.

So, Leonard, descendent of high Hebrew priests, having washed Westmount out of his being, quite naturally craves the understanding of the eternal and unites and sings about it. He has shown a faith in the future, in the very act of encouraging his singing son, Adam, to join with him in song.

George Steiner, an extraordinary eloquent philosopher commented: "From the unreasoned analyzable, often ruinous all-power of love stems the thought that 'God' is not yet. That he will come into being or, more precisely, into manifest reach of human perception, only when there is immense excess and every injustice inflicted on man or beast justifies the findings of atheism in so far as it prevents God from what would indeed be a first coming. But I am unable, even at the worst hours, to abdicate from the belief that the two validating wonders of mortal existence are love and the invention of the future tense. Their conjunction, if it will ever come to pass, is the Messianic."

Amen!

I long for the day when Leonard and I, searching souls, can put on our prayer shawls and pray and, yes, sing together in Hebrew, *Modeh ani lefanecha* — Lord, I thank you for the new day in which I may learn and play and laugh...

> *And those who dance begin to dance*
> *Those who weep begin*
> *And those who earnestly are lost*
> *Are lost and lost again*

* * *

And now there is the singing voice at the other end of the phone, gravel and honey and passion and fun. "*Yom Kippur Ha'zeh*...This is Leonard. I've called you to wish you a healthy New Year." Mortality was very much on our minds in the autumn of 2000. Leonard and I had separately become friends of Pierre Trudeau. Somehow we were all connected, by style, aspiration, a definite lust for life and in this time of our lives a dedication to children. Old Testament style patriarchs, we three. The puzzle of how to raise children and keep them free of the glare of public attention after you have achieved a certain fame or notoriety.

For me personally, it had taken the form of what I enjoyed calling "lunch at the summit." Each year, on the opening day of the Montreal International Film Festival, Trudeau and I would meet for an Asian meal and he would join me for the world premier of my latest film. It was a matter of personal pride that the former and most articulate of our country's leaders would take the time to share the experience. Sometimes Pierre would bring one of his sons along and I would bring Adam, my son, who was studying medicine in Montreal. We enjoyed the continuity, the link in our beliefs as personified in our children. It gave meaning to our existence, there in flesh and blood.

Trudeau was a devout man, his basic belief shattered by the accidental death of his youngest son, an avalanche gone wild. God avenging what?

I recall at lunch one time trying to comfort him with a poem by Emily Bronte, *With Courage to Endure*. But who could endure what was unendurable? I told him of the Hebrew custom of mourning — a year for a parent, a month for a spouse, forever for a child.

And it was forever for him. I watched the life, the youth, drain from him. Comfort? I really don't know.

I was not surprised to hear of his death. This man who seemed to personify the best of the country, its youth, its wildness, its raw adventure. He was gone and so much of ourselves with him. The mediocre was left, our challenge diminished without our leader. The poetry of our soul, endangered.

The only one of my films Trudeau had asked to keep was *The Song of Leonard Cohen*. He and his sons had worn it thin, he once told me.

So, I was not surprised to learn that the boys had asked Leonard to be an honorary pallbearer. Many would not understand. But Trudeau was always in search of the poetry of the soul. The gentle waves of the canoe were a kind of music he cherished. The northern forests were jagged lyrics, the landscape of his very being.

I was not astonished when Leonard told me Trudeau, in his dying days, had asked him to read a poem he had written about death, over and over. Although Trudeau was a devout Catholic and carried with him his basic faith, he turned to his Jewish friends for a kind of poetic comfort — to Leonard in his questing songs and poems and to the penetrating sound of Barbara Striesand. Yes, people really do need people!

Leonard had, of course, written and rewritten that splendid Hebrew prayer of the Day of Atonement, *Who by Fire?* A chronicle of who might survive the coming year, and whose name would be contained in the book of life. "Lord give me another year, another season to taste the goodness of the morning, the pleasure of the day, the love of family."

We talked of these things, the things that linked us, the laughs we enjoyed, the passion for creation. Leonard and I talked of many things.

Leonard told me that each Friday night he lit the Sabbath candles with his children, as I did with my wonderful wife. We held on to each other with thoughts and words and silences. And I heard his song once again...

THE DYLAN DIARIES
A Song Never Sung, Circa 1966

Let us now compare mythologies, as Leonard would say. Since the comparison of Leonard to Dylan has been made so often. Perhaps, if I spell out my experience with Dylan, you will forgive this literary detour. The story is contained in what became The Dylan Diaries *written several years ago, but now published here for the first time. Be patient reading them, suffer along with me. The time is 1966 or thereabout.*

"Dylan!"

First there was the word.

"Ever hear of Bob Dylan?" The voice of my agent, Bernie Wintraub of G.A.C., on my Manhattan apartment phone was both a question and a challenge. "Sure I've heard of him. He's a weird folk singer. I read a piece about him in *The New York Times*. Some people say he's a poet. Some people say he's a nut and some a genius. So what?"

It was the evening of Passover and I was preparing to drive my wife and daughter Holly, age four months, out to my brother's on Long Island. It seemed like a normal, folksy thing to do. As it turned out, the last one act of calmness in sometime to come.

("Lord, why is this night different than all other nights?" — I was about to find out).

"I've recommended you as the producer of a one-hour television special on ABC about Dylan." Bernie's voice rose a little, as the enthusiasm of his apparent act of faith became punctuation.

"A musical?" Since I had just returned from Vietnam it seemed a fair question.

"No. Yes. No, not exactly. At any rate you may have to leave right away for Australia. And then round the world...and then.."

"Hold on. It's Passover tonight. I can't go to Australia."

"I don't mean leave tonight. But you may have to meet Dylan's manager. He's leaving for the Coast tonight and then Australia and the world. And he may want you to go."

"Okay, okay. I'll go to Australia, but after the Seder tonight. All right? If I don't leave now I'll get stuck on the Long Island Expressway and I'll never get as far as Rockville Centre which is where my brother lives on the way to Australia."

"Look. You hold on there. I'll get Lester Gotlieb, the agent who is handling this to get the manger and maybe you can meet with him before he takes off. Could be a big show. And Dylan is hot."

I calmed my wife who was calming my child who was already dressed for her long expedition to Long Island. There were hostile looks from both.

"But Bernie says Dylan is hot." I tried to explain.

"Your baby is hot," said my normally patient, pleasant wife. "You've just come back from Vietnam, and now you're going to Australia?"

"But Vietnam was where the war was. This is different. Could be fun. Music and..." I tried a soft shoe shuffle and waited. We could see darkness coming as we waited and the baby who seemed to be expressing her own ideas wet her diaper twice.

After an hour the phone rang. It was Bernie. "Couldn't find the manager. Better go enjoy Passover and check with us tomorrow."

I thought it odd at the time that they couldn't find Dylan's manager and that he should be leaving for a round the world trip without having made arrangements for a producer for an important TV special.

"Run," I said to myself. "Run." But stuck on the long Island Expressway for two hours because our trip had been delayed and my child crying all the way through the "Four Questions" and during gefilte fish there was little chance to run. The hot horseradish seemed especially bitter that night.

The next day I met at the G.A.C. offices, sort of imitation early American which is sort of late M.C.A., with Lester Gotlieb, a pleasant avuncular agent whose blasé expression seemed to be permanent as a result of witnessing several decades of show business behind the scars.

"I'm trying to get Albert Grossman, Dylan's manager, on the phone so we can fly out to meet with him in L.A."

Gotlieb studied my credits. I'd been producing, directing and writing documentaries of all kinds all round the world for half a dozen networks for a dozen years. From difficult situations, I liked to think, I could bring education and entertainment and beauty. I had followed Fidel Castro through wild, Cuban nights, had politely directed Lady Bird in take after take during a humid Washington summer, been lowered from a helicopter over the South China seas off the Coast of Vietnam and had pushed my way across the entire continent of Africa. Dylan was another kind of story and I was curious!

Four days went by. I decided to forget the film and was planning another show in Westminster Abbey in London. Thursday night, April 7, just before midnight the phone rang. My baby cried. It was Gotlieb. "Grossman says come to Hollywood. Dylan will see you tomorrow. They're leaving for Honolulu tomorrow night."

Gotlieb checked into the Beverly Hills Hotel. I decided to go to the Continental Hotel where Grossman was staying. It seemed democratic somehow, even if the Continental was a local Hollywood hangout for musicians, staying at a special reduction from Gene Autrey who sang and smiled his way to millions on a horse.

Albert Grossman, manager to Bob Dylan and other singers like Peter, Paul and Mary, was reputed to have made millions, from the teenage folk and folk-rock world. Now, at the Continental Hotel, he greeted me as Dylan records scratched away on a portable record player. Grossman, obvious believer of being Roman in Rome, wore his gray hair in the longhaired tradition of the modern music movement. The carefully brushed flowing locks give him a look that was somewhere between Ben Franklin and your Aunt Fannie. He stared from behind metal-rimmed glasses as if he was enjoying his own private secret.

"Dylan someday will be remembered the same way as Shelley and Keats."

(To myself I said, "Run. Run.")

To Grossman I said, "Really. That's marvelous." Grossman put on another record. I couldn't hear the lyrics even though I was sober.

After Gotlieb and I said it was "interesting," Grossman swung the dial of a portable radio. He found Dylan three times. I was impressed but wondered what Percy Byshe Shelley and John Keats would have thought about it. It wasn't exactly *Ozymandias*.

Gotlieb had to attend another meeting in town with Pat Boone. I listened to more Dylan until the original arrived. Half a dozen men with hair poured into the room. One with high purple suede shoes and corduroy all over, from behind large black glasses said, "Man, what you got for the stomach and head."

"Mr. Rasky, this is Bob Dylan."

("Catch the next plane," I said to myself.)

"I think I have some gelusil," I said to Dylan.

His handshake was like limp lettuce. He took off his glasses. There was a moment, maybe a second, I liked. Deep in those eyes, below that hostile hair, I saw a look. It was pain and love and fear and hurt and a strange tenderness. It was a boy crouching out of a rainstorm somehow saying, "Don't hit me again." It was an alley kitten that wants to be noticed or caressed. It was awful aloneness. And then I never saw that look again.

But in that fragment of time I saw the runaway. As the stories go he was born in Duluth, Minnesota on May 24, 1941 and tried to run away almost as soon as he could walk. And run and run again. He ran from the dead town in which he was reared, Hibbing. And ran from his name and family which is supposed to have been the poor white slave of poverty. Now he was the rich master.

"I don't know why you're here, man," he barked.

"I'm a writer, director and producer."

"I don't need no writer, director and producer."

And that's the way the conversation and adventure began. What followed could have been done nicely by the Marx brothers. In fact, I think it was. A young man, if anything thinner than Dylan, came into the room, his head hidden beneath a dark tam.

"I don't believe it man. What did you do to your hair?"

Apparently he had been with Dylan's group and had cut his lengthy curls.

"It's just that I been home in Texas, and they didn't dig hair."

"It's okay, man, I got a wig."

Room service came and went six times. Cokes and ice tea and lobster. And four musicians spread out on the bed listening to records of Dylan playing *Rainy Day Women #12 and #35* (with the lyrics, 'Everybody must get stoned...') And the poor boy hiding his hair that he had lost in a square Texas town.

Cameraman D.A. Pennebaker who specializes in Cinema Verité, an expression that can mean for some the hand-held truth or for others sloppy out of focus shooting, rushed in the room and said he needed a shave.

I asked Dylan what he thought of the Beatles' movies and would he like his special to be the same.

"No, man, there are four of them. Just one of me." I asked him what he thought his film should say. "Say, man. It doesn't have to say anything."

I asked him if he thought it should be entertaining. "What's entertaining, man? Don't you see, it's got to be something. Not like that Barbara Streisand stuff. I mean this is going to be like something never before done."

"But what?"

"I don't know. How can I know now!"

All the time he talked his leg twitched and he smoked continuously. His fingers so stained with nicotine they looked like crooked twigs.

A conference with his manager in the washroom followed. "Look man, I don't know who you are or what you're doing here," he said after they came out of the toilet. "If the network wants you to come and watch us film you get your bread. But I don't need you. I don't care who you are. I've got no time."

I tried to explain that he, in fact, had paid for my ticket to the Coast.

"Look, if I want a director I could call Marlon Brando. He's got a bigger name that you."

His manager suggested Brando might be busy.

Now he was a wild, hostile alley cat. For a moment I had an urge to spank him. But you don't spank stars, I told myself. He scratched the air with his voice and pulled himself within himself. I had asked questions and Dylan had begun running again. Somehow I had begun to represent authority in his mind. The enemy, the past. He didn't want to stay in the room with me.

"See you in Copenhagen," were my last words to him.

If I was to produce the show, it was agreed that is where the filming would begin, three weeks later.

What followed was a chase across capitals and continents. Kafka took hold of a situation that was unpredictable.

Manager Grossman said he would let me know from Honolulu if we were going ahead. That weekend I received conflicting advice from some of my best professional friends.

Norman Jewison, a former college-mate and then director of *The Russians are Coming, The Russians are Coming*, said, "Dylan is one of the great young performers of our time." Arthur Hiller, with whom I worked at the CBC in Canada, said, "Life is too short."

When I returned to New York, I still had heard no word and once again tried to put the project out of my mind. It was difficult. That moment of awful loneliness I had seen in Dylan's eyes seemed to haunt me. In many ways my own life had recently changed. I had gone to Vietnam and had seen at close range the madness of war. I saw young men in battle and found that some enjoyed the horror of war and others were sleepwalkers through foreign battle. Coca-Cola in Mekong Delta and a ride by helicopter as the pilot pointed his machine gun at the rice paddies below as I listened to *Days of Wine and Roses* on the intercom. American civilization as represented by the President and his stubborn policy seemed as mad as the mad scenes at the Continental Hotel.

I searched for comments in the works of Dylan. In some of his lyrics I could feel the honest anger of youth. In his *Masters of War* there was the kind of terror I had felt in Vietnam and seen in young faces.

The words were strong, and angry, but not really poetic and I discovered a great darkness about many of the songs. If Dylan was indeed protesting injustice he only seemed to want to answer with vengeance. It seemed like a young boy rebuking a parent with, "I hope you die."

I could recall college magazines used to carry some of this kind of material. But in the post-second world war days when I was at school the world was spinning in a more optimistic orbit, even if it was after Hiroshima. Now in the Vietnam decade, the Dylan timing was perfect. If human history had led up to the obscenity of that incredible war, no wonder he had an audience of protest. But two things were missing from the historical ballads that made them a part of American folklore: Love and hope. Nothing in Dylan had that.

And then, despite his success there was the question of whether he should be taken seriously at all. One of his strongest admirers had been Robert Shelton of *The New York Times* who has called Dylan, "The pioneer...the trail-blazer and the innovator." Well, certainly Dylan had put his college magazine poetry to music. And he was making a loud noise.

Commentator or clown, thousands still knew his name and even if what he was representing was just vague anarchy, it proved that a lot of young people could find some kind of therapy in his confusing metaphors and attitudes. And there was money in it.

After a week, word came from Australia for me to join the troupe in Europe. I had heard that the Australian part of the tour had been something of a disaster. Crowds had been sparse and Dylan had, according to *Variety*, antagonized the press with his "put-on" answers.

It was a change from the tours of triumph he had been experiencing. It had not gone over Down Under.

Meantime it had been agreed in New York that Pennebaker would provide the crew for the Dylan TV special. He had done a two hour film the year before of a Dylan tour and had gained Dylan's confidence. His soundman was to be a leggy blonde by the name of Jones — her first name was Jones.

"Penny" and I held a brief discussion in New York about our approach to the subject. We were wide apart but it seemed possible to work together. For the Cinema Verité bugs the camera must never intrude. Lighting must never intrude. Sound must never intrude. It has always been my feeling that all filmmaking in a sense is a lie, and therefore, there is a conflict of terms. The minute a picture is framed, something been has left out or selectively included. When a film is edited it takes advantage of the mind which tricks the eye. Thus Cinema Verité is, in a sense, the greatest lie of all — it follows people down corridors as if the camera-man had a limp because its felt wheels would intrude...it catches backs of heads which is seldom the way we see reality in reality... it dwells on out of focus photography because nothing has been planned ahead. But we do see objects in focus unless we are myopic and have lost our glasses. To me filming had always meant the creative look at reality...substance of the senses arranged to produce an emotion.

Despite all differences we said we would meet in London in early May because it was difficult to get the camera crew ready for Scandinavia.

London was springtime. Despite the recent *TIME* article which had dubbed London "the swinging city" the old London was still there. Beefeaters were still wisecracking their way around tours of the Tower of London and treating old King Henry as if he died yesterday morning. At the theatre there were still drinks or tea at the "interval." And Westminster Abbey with its gothic majesty was having a birthday party — nine hundred years old if it's a day. A city crusted with tradition awaited a young singer and friends whose songs and attitudes proclaimed all history so far was leading to oblivion.

I waited at London's plush May Fair Hotel for the Dylan group to make a stop on their way back from Australia. On the last tour everyone had checked in at the Savoy. The Savoy strangely said it had no rooms this time, despite the fact several other people I knew had registered.

Word came from the Tito Burns office, the European arrangers of the tour, the group would go directly to Stockholm. I tried phoning Dylan and Grossman daily to see if I should join them in Stockholm. The calls were never answered. Then they were to move on to Copenhagen for an overnight concert. They could not be reached.

Three days later the group arrived in London. I looked up from my afternoon tea in the lobby of the May Fair to see a small dark man come shooting across the lobby. A hushed conference followed. Dylan and two of his musical group scampered across the lobby, as if avoiding autograph seekers. There were no auto no autograph seekers. A giant limousine and cockney chauffeur were parked outside.

Half an hour later the film crew led by Pennebaker in a cliché gray top hat pulled up in another limousine. I was told he had just returned from Scandinavia where he had exposed five thousand feet of color film.

The only comment: "It was wild." No explanation. Manager Grossman had gone on to Berlin or Paris or someplace.

Half an hour later I walked into suite 124 where Dylan was staying. He sat collapsed into a couch wearing dark glasses. He sat in his corduroy purple pants, his shoes off, his feet on a table. His toes danced a nervous twitch.

"Hello there. Welcome to London," I said with what now seems like foolish friendliness.

Dylan looked up, peered through his dark glasses, and managed a reluctant nod. He switched television channels. He sent for six magazines at the lobby stand.

"I can't go out in London," he said to one of half a dozen young men with hair in the room, all slouching in armchairs.

I had seen Lorne Greene, with whom I had worked for several years, in the lobby. Sitting about were Don Blocker, *Bonanza's* Hoss, Tony Randall, and Sammy Davis Jr. The night before I had seen Glenn Ford who had narrated my latest film on Vietnam at a Noel Coward play. All seemed to be able to "go out in London."

Jones, the leggy soundman smiled a greeting. Half a dozen magazines arrived and Dylan seemed to consume them at once.

Dylan looked up to say to no one in particular, "Hey, listen to this, man, a guy says 'I'd rather die then have my daughter marry a 'nigger." How about that! Right here in this magazine."

Dylan switched channels again. The BBC was showing a series called *All Our Yesterdays*, about the Second World War. At one point a Swastika was raised.

"Hey look at that. It's groovy. I'd love to have one of those," one of the musicians said.

As Pennebaker reached for the phone Dylan finished his sixth magazine in about six minutes, "Hey, man, don't use the phone. Marlon (Brando) might be calling."

Brando never called.

Next morning I drove out to Ealing studios where I watched my friend Bob Parish skillfully direct immense Orson Welles in a scene from Ian Fleming's *Casino Royale*. I envied the professional attitude in the studio, and exchanged some small talk with Welles, who somehow had lost his wardrobe that morning — hard to duplicate at his current girth. I told him I had been filming at the Hearst mansion earlier in the year and that they "thought fondly" of him there. He allowed a large Vincent Price laugh.

I arrived back at the May Fair in time for a two-thirty press conference with Dylan which began at three.

A dozen photographers circled round him and flashed and popped.

"Suck your glasses would you," said one.

"You suck them," said Dylan offering him glasses.

"Suck a cigarette," another ordered.

"Cross your legs. That's right."

"How about a profile by the window?"

With a look of playful contempt Dylan climbed out of the window onto the ledge. Several photographers followed.

When Dylan came in from the ledge the reporters filled the room. Unlike his tour of a year before there were none from the daily London press. All were from music papers and some hangers on.

Dylan insisted on turning the radio on while the press

conference was being held. He seemed to always need background sound. Silence seemed an enemy. He looked through his dark glasses and played with the press.

"What is your new group called, Bob?"

"They are not called anything."

"Why are your songs unrelated to the titles?"

"No reason."

"Do you have a new wife?"

"I'd be a liar if I answered that."

"Shall we assume you are married?"

"You can assume anything you like."

"Surely you must know whether or not you're married?"

"I was born married."

"It says in the press release you've written a book. What is it about?"

"It's about spiders."

"Spiders?"

"Yes, it's about tarantulas."

"You no longer seem to sing protest songs."

"Like what?"

"Like you used to sing."

"You name it and I'll protest against it."

Once or twice Dylan broke the pattern of giving nonsense answers to insignificant questions.

When he was asked if he preferred Britain to America he said, "No, I prefer America because America is what I know." When he was asked if he was bitter because of his childhood he said, "Where I come from there were no rich people. I didn't know I was poor until I left there."

He was asked if he had any possessions. Money, some said, had been an embarrassment to this young protester. In his answer he was off again, running, putting everyone on, running.

"Oh, yes, I own an airport in San Diego. And I intend to buy all the Mormons."

A year earlier at the same press conference he had been asked if he believed in anything and he had answered, "No I don't believe in anything. Why should I?"

Whatever he did believe in was his private secret with himself.

On one subject though, he was open and interested. The question of modern music. When he was asked how it was that Britain seemed to be leading the way, he dropped his "camp." He said that when the Beatles were born, there was just no one in America who was leading any kind of musical movement. And thus the winds of change came west across the Atlantic instead of the traditional direction. But now, he indicated, that had changed. Among the Beatles, who he either likes or envies, it was John Lennon, the creative writer, who he sought out. He cared about what Lennon had to say about music.

When the press conference was over he attacked one of the reporters with, "If you haven't studied music what right do you have to write about it?"

As the reporters left for a final drink he turned to someone to ask, "Have they been told, all the concerts are sold out."

But the reporters were gone and in the background the radio was playing a pre-Dylan, *Going to Take a Sentimental Journey*.

Dylan decided to go out and do some filming around London. Pennebaker suggested I not come along as Dylan got tight inside when I was around.

In the lobby I tapped Dylan on the shoulder and suggested I come along. "No man, you can't do that. This is private filming. You can go to concerts and things." And he pulled himself inside himself and I stared at the wild hair which seemed a hiding place.

There were a couple of all-nighters on the town and a limousine driver who promised never to tell. In London then, talent was the new royalty. And the young performers had taken on the private all- nighters of revelry once reserved for dukes and such. They floated around the clubs in shaded cars like olives in search of so many martinis. Their escapades were largely unrecorded except for the occasional gossip columnists. Their dawn was mid-day and the fun began past mid-night. And their code was signified by a sign outside a hotel room door that said, "Do not disturb."

As for me, I waited for the arrival of manager Al Grossman who showed up past midnight two days later.

"I'll let you know," he said.

In the morning he called from the lobby to say, "You might as well take some time off."

"How long?" I asked.

"Oh, a couple weeks."

"The way things are going," I said, "you might end up with twenty hours of home movies."

Grossman thought that was funny. But I was prophetically correct. I decided to send for my wife and take off for Malaga in Spain. If there was going to be blood on the sand I wanted it to be at a bullfight in which the only victim was a bull.

The group went to Dublin and Belfast. Apparently Dylan had been pounding a piano in the early hours of the morning in Belfast and the pilot of a plane, in the next room, complained about the racket. Dylan and a buddy jumped on a plane and tried to get back to London in the middle of the night. The plane developed engine trouble and it was mid-day before Dylan arrived back...apparently in the style of Durante, looking for that lost chord. If once he had a wanderer by thumb and rail now he had planes at his disposal. He could run round the world now, and faster, faster, like a rollin' stone.

On a rainy Sunday while I was sitting in room 111 at the May Fair, in Pennebaker's room, Dylan came in wearing a borrowed pair of ladies flower coloured bell-bottom slacks.

"These are great," he said. "I can wear two pair of my pants underneath."

He caught sight of a large brown cigar I was smoking. He asked me if I had another. I went to my room and I got him one. I also got my raincoat as it was decided there would be some filming in Hyde Park.

When he saw I had my coat and intended to go along he stepped into the hall. Jones, the leggy soundman, was in the hall with him and returned to the room.

"Dylan says here's your cigar back."

Dylan did not want to have any obligation. He took a tambourine and set out for Speaker's Corner.

Some of Dylan's critics had said he no longer seemed interested in songs of social meaning and had turned to ballads like *Mr. Tambourine Man.*

The Dylan group wandered around the ancient empty streets of London. I listened to one tape from Speaker's Corner where Dylan engaged in dialogue with some anarchists and then proceeded to strip down his borrowed flowery pants.

Out of the rumble and chaos of Jones' sound came a voice, "How could you, the greatest protester, become one of the worst defeatists."

And a slurred answer, "I don't know. I don't know."

There were a couple more brief encounters. When my wife arrived I took her into Dylan's room where a party was going on. There was a girl who had come the previous day from Denmark when Dylan had said "Come to London," and a lot of long-haired young men, smoky haze and rocking music blaring from a tape recorder, a Beatle or two, pale lip-sticked young girls sitting on the floor.

"It's *Marat/Sade,*" my wife said. "That's the scene we saw in the play."

Marat/Sade takes place in a madhouse.

The night before Malaga, when Dylan was to take off for Bristol, there was a darkened limousine outside the May Fair.

The doorman said, "I don't know who it is. I think it's the Rolling Stones or some of those queer birds. They all had hair."

The Beatles had come to call and the constant beat of music crept from below the sign that read "Do not disturb."

It was announced that there would be a screening of the two-hour film made of Dylan's tour of the year before in the May Fair Cinema in the basement. A week before, Sammy Davis Jr. had rented it for a nocturnal screening of horror films.

At two-thirty in the morning the movie house filled with assorted Beatles, beards and girls in mini-skirts. Ringo looked like a wedding cake doll version of himself. He seemed to have shrunk. But I guess he was always small. Dylan sat in the row behind me with John Lennon, his feet drooped over the row ahead. He had not slept in two nights. And behind his dark glasses his pale complexion seemed so white it was almost like clown make-up.

The curtains parted and for two hours the film went on. Dylan at press conferences, on trains and in cars, being mobbed somewhat out of focus, a blurred Joan Baez singing in a hotel room, a scratched Albert Hall concert all ending in a scene where a review was being read to Dylan calling him "an anarchist."

The elderly woman in the next seat whispered to me, "Rubbish. It's all rubbish."

A voice from the back called out, "Hey, that's a groovy flick man. Real groovy."

There had been several mentions of the Beatles in the picture. They stood and said nothing. Nothing.

The film was over and we all started to leave. The dozen or so hangers-on, who were travelling in the Dylan orbit, somehow making some kind of time or money out of the Dylan legend.

Everyone was leaving, but Dylan was still sitting there, draped over two rows, a faint, faded figure under a burden of hair, alone.

As an afterthought, almost, it was noticed Dylan had not risen. "Hey Bobby, wake up. It's over. It's all over. The flick is finished,"one of the long-haired boys said.

He looked a little startled. Where was he? A boy of obscure beginnings, twenty-five years old in a few days, who had traveled a million miles across a frozen wasteland, alone, alone, who had made a million dollars worth of protest, was wakened in his own rented theatre alone. The flick was over.

I did not see Dylan after that.

In the time with Dylan, I had seen the grown men-in-waiting and the children at the gate who seemed to say, "Bobby tell us what to think." T.S. Elliot captured a mood with poetic eloquence:

> For children at the gate
> Who will not go away and cannot pray
> Pray for these who chose and oppose
> O my people what have I done.

I have of course thought about him since the time I began to record *The Dylan Diaries*. Perhaps what Dylan was all about was that grown men no longer had a message for the young. In the Vietnam age it was hard to explain a sense of values. Had centuries of tradition merely led to the time of atomic waste?

Or maybe in those affluent times it was a period to put college magazine poetry to music. Kids could pay to hear it now.

It is of course also possible that Dylan was putting us all on. At a time when soup cartons go for art, Batman for mass culture, and blobs on film for skill, maybe Dylan had lost respect for people who would pay well to hear the bawlings of a boy.

Whatever Dylan was I can tell you he was running hard and long and fast...within himself...running hard and long inside.

I tried to catch him. I don't know if I did.

I'm not sure Dylan is either lost or found.

As for me, I went on to Spain, returned to London and then

New York. Since then I have thought about something Albert Grossman, Dylan's father-figure manager, said to me when he was encouraging me to take on the job as producer of the TV special. "You can be sure you'll get something out of this trip, even if it's not what you expected."

Bob Dylan, Hello and Goodbye.

*   *   *

But of course it was not the end. Re-reading these diaries many years later, I find I am still pained by the experience. Many people have asked, 'what happened to the film?' I was right about that — it was never seen. Dylan fired Pennebaker, edited it himself, fell off a motorcycle and did, indeed, become a kind of spokesman for the age of rage. He was angry. He stayed angry. It chills me now as it chilled me then.

The $100,000 advance that Albert Goldman had received from ABC had to be returned. I have never seen a frame of the film.

Dylan continued to prowl and scowl, to rant and rave, his energy dedicated to tearing away at the system. It was all a horror, right? What did the past have to say or teach or preach? *Gimme Shelter*. (I note in passing and without comment that when the Kennedy Center in Washington offered him its honors at the hand of the pudgy, President he accepted without protest.)

I took shelter, refuge, in the beauty of the past where I could find it. For me it was the Poet's Corner in Westminster Abbey in London. If the times were drowning Browning, boiling the Brontes, I relished in them. And then with the mellow, sophisticated delight of the mellifluous sound of James Mason as guide I created *Hall of Kings*, one of my finest hours, my first Emmy and the rebirth of my own self-worth, almost squashed by the stinging power of Dylan and the forces let loose at that time.

Yes, it was a time of horror. I had been to Vietnam, and sent letters home to my new daughter, Holly, that were published around the world. I was an early protester of that ugly, little divisive war. Its stupidity only increased the influence of Dylan, which was vast. And those terrible assassinations in America and riots were somehow more than we could handle.

Burn baby, burn became a call to arms. Where was beauty, tradition and love? How could we rescue meaning for ourselves?

I had to surrender my beloved New York and return to Canada where I was offered the opportunity at the time to make films that concentrated on lasting, poetic values. No holds barred. No interference. Create what I could. Experiment. It was as if I had swallowed the universe whole. G. Bernard Shaw who found humor in the horror of men, but also redemption, provided a kind of code to emulate and never forget, in words from my first film for the CBC:

"I believe in Michelangelo, Velasquez and Rembrandt, in the might of design, the mystery of color, the redemption of things by beauty everlasting, and the message of art that made these hands blessed."

And so now I especially honor the time I spent with Leonard Cohen — trying in my way to be free.

Index of First Lines

AGMV Marquis

MEMBER OF SCABRINI MEDIA

Quebec, Canada
2002